Financial Astrology
Almanac
2016

M. G. BUCHOLTZ, B.Sc., MBA

Wood Dragon Books

Box 1216, Regina, Saskatchewan, Canada, S4P 3B4

www.wooddragonbooks.com

ISBN# 978-0-9948700-1-8

Financial Astrology Almanac 2016

Copyright 2015 Malcolm Bucholtz, B.Sc., MBA

Printed in Canada

CONTENTS

FIGURES

ACKNOWLEDGMENTS

To my beautiful wife, Jeanne, who continues to inspire me in so many ways and without whose encouragement my published books would not have become reality.

Disclaimer

All material provided herein is based on material gleaned from mathematical and astrological publications researched by the author to supplement his own trading. This publication is written with sincere intent for those who actively trade and invest in the financial markets and who are looking to incorporate astrological phenomena and esoteric math into their market activity. While the material presented herein has proven reliable to the author in his personal trading and investing activity, there is no guarantee the material herein will continue to be reliable into the future. The author and publisher assume no liability whatsoever for any investment or trading decisions made by readers of this book. The reader alone is responsible for all trading and investment outcomes and is further advised not to exceed his or her risk tolerances when trading or investing on the financial markets.

Recommended Readings

The Bull, the Bear and the Planets, M.G. Bucholtz, (iUniverse, USA, 2013)

The Lost Science, M.G. Bucholtz, (iUniverse, USA, 2013)

The Universal Clock, J. Long, (P.A.S. Publishing, USA,)

McWhirter Theory of Stock Market Forecasting, L. McWhirter, (Astro Book Company, USA, 1938)

The Universe Within, N. Turok, (House of Anansi Press, Canada, 2012)

A Theory of Continuous Planet Interaction, Tony Waterfall, NCGR Research Journal, Volume 4, Spring 2014, pp67-87.

INTRODUCTION

Many market analysts and financial media commentators think daily news, quarterly earnings reports and corporate events drive stock prices.

I disagree.

There is something else that drives the financial markets. I have two opinions on what this something else might be.

The first opinion is that the financial markets are a reflection of the mass psychological emotion of traders, investors and fund managers. The term *reflection* may even be too mild of a descriptor. It may be more accurate to boldly state that human emotion drives buying and selling decisions in the financial markets. When market participants are feeling positive, they are driven to buy. When they are feeling uncertain or negative, they are driven to sell.

Probing this idea deeper immediately yields the complex question - what drives human emotion?

Medical researchers still have not definitively answered this question. Some say changes in blood alkalinity or acidity impact our emotions. Some say changes in chemical hormones in the bloodstream are the cause. My humble opinion on this complex matter is that the ever-changing configurations of orbiting planets and other celestial bodies in our cosmos influence our body chemistry and thereby drive human emotion.

This opinion has been shaped by the many Astrology publications I have read over the past several years including Tony Waterfall's insightful article from the Spring 2014 NCGR Research Journal. In his article Waterfall reminds readers that the Sun is the centre of our planetary system. The Sun emits massive amounts of solar radiation in all directions into the vastness of space. This radiation is called *solar wind*. This solar wind interacts with the magnetic fields around Mercury, Venus, Moon, Mars, Jupiter, Saturn, Uranus, Neptune and Pluto. These planets accept and then disburse the solar wind radiation. As the radiation is disbursed, a goodly amount of it finds its way towards the magnetic field around planet Earth. Changes in the density and speed of solar wind mean that the amount of radiation reaching Earth's magnetic field on a daily, weekly or monthly basis will be ever-changing. As a result, the intensity or flux of the Earth's magnetic field is also constantly changing. The alignment of the orbiting planets at any given time in our cosmos plays a key role in determining how much solar radiation is deflected towards Earth's magnetic field. A simplistic way of viewing this entire arrangement is to think of a billiards table as the cosmos. The various balls on the table are the planets and other celestial bodies. The solar radiation is the white cue ball bouncing and deflecting off other balls on the table. The human body is largely comprised of water. We all have an electrical field that runs through our tissues. Hence, basic physics demands that changes to the Earth's magnetic field will then induce subtle changes to our bodily electric circuitry. These subtle changes, in my opinion, are what drive our emotional responses. But there is so much more to be understood. Scientists and psychologists who are on a quest to learn more have come to call the developing science of how the cosmos affects humans *cosmo-biology*.

Ancient civilizations as far back as the Babylonians too recognized cosmo-biology, but in a more rudimentary form. Their high priests tracked and recorded changes in the emotions of the people. These diviners and seers tracked events, both fortuitous and disastrous. Although they lacked the ability to comprehend the physics of solar wind and magnetic fields, they were able to visually spot planets Mercury, Venus, Mars, Jupiter and Saturn in the heavens. They correlated changes in human emotion and changes in societal events to these planets. They assigned to these planets the names of the various Deities revered by the people. They further identified and named various star constellations in the heavens and further divided the heavens into twelve signs. This was the birth of Astrology as we know it today.

Starting in the early 1900's, esoteric thinkers such as the famous Wall Street trader W.D. Gann noted that basic Astrology bore a striking correlation to changes on the financial markets. This was the birth of financial Astrology. Gann based his writings and forecasts on the synodic cycles between various planets. Gann also delved deep into esoteric math, notably square root math. He is well remembered for Gann Lines – a technique based on square roots. But Gann lived in a challenging time. Statute laws in places like New York expressly forbade the use of occult science in business ventures. Gann therefore carefully concealed the basis for his market forecasts. Today many traders and investors try to emulate Gann but they do so in a linear fashion – looking for repetitive cycles on the calendar. What they are missing is the Astrology component, which is anything but linear.

In the 1930s, Louise McWhirter followed closely in Gann's footsteps. She identified an 18.6 year cyclical correlation between the general state of the American economy and the position of the North Node of Moon. Her methodology also extended to include the Moon passing by key points of the 1792 natal birth horoscope of the New York Stock Exchange. As well, she identified a correlation between price movement of a stock and those times when transiting Sun, Mars, Jupiter and Saturn made hard aspects to the natal Sun position in the stock's natal birth horoscope.

The late 1940s saw even further advancements in the field of financial Astrology when astrologer Garth Allen (a.k.a. Donald Bradley) produced his Siderograph Model. This complex model is based on aspects between the various transiting planets. Each aspect as it occurs is given a sinusoidal weighting as the *orb* between the planets varies. This model is as powerful today as it was in the late 1940s.

My second opinion on what drives financial markets is a brazen one. This opinion bluntly says that the markets are manipulated from deep within New York, London and other financial centers. This manipulation is based around astrological cycles and occurrences. It is then quite possible that once efforts to "move" the markets are underway at these various points in time, human emotion kicks in and media frenzy takes over. As you read these words, I invite you to think back to August 2015 and the market selloff that apparently nobody saw coming. The reality is that this selloff started at a confluence of three events. August 2015 marked a cyclical 180 degree advancement of heliocentric Venus, a Venus retrograde event and the appearance of Venus as a morning star after having been only visible as an evening star for the past 263 days.

I personally began to embrace financial Astrology in 2012 which was a monumental shift given that my educational background comprises an Engineering degree and an MBA degree. Two linear-thinking, left brain degrees to be sure. Since 2012, my research and back-testing has satisfied me that a correlation does indeed exist between Astrology and the financial markets. This Almanac represents my sixth publication on the subject of financial Astrology.

This Almanac begins by offering you a fairly thorough look at the cyclical math and science of Astrology. What then follows is an examination of the New York Stock Exchange for the twelve months of calendar year 2016. Each monthly examination presents a summation of key dates when Astrology events stand a high probability of influencing human emotion. A look at various commodity futures and the astro phenomena that influence them then follows. Finally, I provide a look at Gann Lines and also Quantum Price Lines, two esoteric mathematical concepts that should be used when applying Astrology to make trading and investing decisions.

When applying Astrology to trading and investing, it is vital at all times to be aware of the price trend. There are many ways of observing trend. My personal experience has shown me that the chart indicators developed by J. Welles Wilder are very effective at identifying trend changes. In particular, the DMI and the Volatility Stop are two indicators that should be taken seriously. As a trader and investor, what you are looking for is a change of trend that aligns to an astro event. When you see the trend change, you should take action. Whether that action is implementing a long position, a short position or just tightening up on a stop loss will depend on your personal appetite for risk and on your investment and trading objectives. Astrology is not about trying to take action at each and every astro event that comes along. Not all astro events are powerful enough to induce a change of trend. Hence, that is why I advise to be alert at each astro event and to keep your eye open for changes in trend. This Almanac is designed to be a resource for you to help you stay abreast of the various astro events that 2016 holds in store.

I sincerely hope after you have applied the material in this Almanac to your trading and investing activity, you will embrace financial Astrology as a valuable tool.

To further set the tone for what you are about to read in this Almanac, I present to you the following quotes on the subject of Astrology:

"An unfailing experience of mundane events in harmony with the changes occurring in the heavens, has instructed and compelled my unwilling belief." (Johannes Kepler – astronomer, mathematician 1571-1630)

"Heaven sends down its good and evil symbols and wise men act accordingly." (Confucius – Chinese philosopher 551-479 BC)

"The controls of life are structured as forms and nuclear arrangements, in relation with the motions of the universe." (Louis Pasteur-scientist 1822-1895)

"Oh the wonderful knowledge to be found in the stars. Even the smallest things are written there...if you had but skill to read." (Ben Franklin-one of the Founding Fathers of America 1706-1790)

"It's common knowledge that a large percentage of Wall Street brokers use Astrology." (Donald Reagan, formerly Ronald Reagan's Chief of Staff)

1. Mundane Astrology

Astrology is an ancient science focused on the correlation between the planets, events of nature and behaviour of mankind. This ancient science is rooted in thousands of years of observation across many civilizations.

- The ancient Sumerians, Akkadians and Babylonians between the 4th and 2nd centuries BC believed the affairs of mankind could be gauged by watching the motions of certain stars and planets. They recorded their predictions and future indications of prosperity and calamity on clay tablets. These early recordings form the foundation of modern day Astrology.
- Ancient Egyptian artifacts show that high priests Petosiris and Necepso who lived during the reign of Ramses II were revered for their knowledge of Astrology. The Egyptian culture is thought to have developed a 12 month x 30 day time keeping method based on the repeated appearances of constellations.
- Ancient Indian and Chinese artifacts reveal that Astrology held an esteemed place in those societies for many thousands of years.
- Hipparchus, Pythagoras and Plato are key names from the Greek era. Historians think Pythagoras assigned mathematical values to the relations between celestial bodies. Plato is thought to have offered up predictions relating celestial bodies to human fates. Hipparchus is thought to have compiled a star catalogue which popularized Astrology.
- In the latter years of the Roman empire, Astrology was used for political gain. Important military figures surrounded themselves with philosophers such as Ptolemy and Valens. In 126 AD, Ptolemy penned four books describing the influence of the stars. His works are collectively called the *Tetrabiblos*. In 160 AD, Valens penned *Anthologies* in which he further summarized the principles of Astrology.

Following the conversion of Emperor Constantine to Christianity in 312 AD, using Astrology for gain became a crime according to the Church of Rome. Astrology then began a slow retreat to the sidelines where for the most part it remains today. Despite Astrology having been sidelined by a Church seeking to protect its authority, Astrology was still used by leading thinkers such as Galileo, Brahe, Nostradamus, Kepler, Bacon and Newton. Thanks to the tenacity of these men, Astrology was prevented from fading away altogether into a distant memory.

The Zodiac

The Sun is at the center of our solar system. The Earth, Moon, planets and various other asteroid bodies complete our planetary system. The various planets and other asteroid bodies rotate 360 degrees around the Sun following a path called the *ecliptic plane* as shown in Figure 1. Earth is slightly tilted (approximately 23 degrees) relative to the ecliptic plane. Projecting the Earth's equator into space produces the *celestial equator plane.* There are two points of intersection between the ecliptic plane and celestial equator plane. These points are commonly called the *vernal equinox* (occurring at March 20th) and the *autumnal equinox (occurring at September 20th).* Dividing the ecliptic plane into twelve equal sections of 30 degrees results in what astrologers call the *zodiac.* The twelve portions of the zodiac have names including Aries, Cancer, Leo and so on. If these names sound familiar, they should. You routinely see all twelve names in the daily horoscope section of your morning newspaper. Figure 2 illustrates a *zodiac wheel.* The starting point or zero degree point of the zodiac wheel is the sign Aries, located at the vernal equinox of each year.

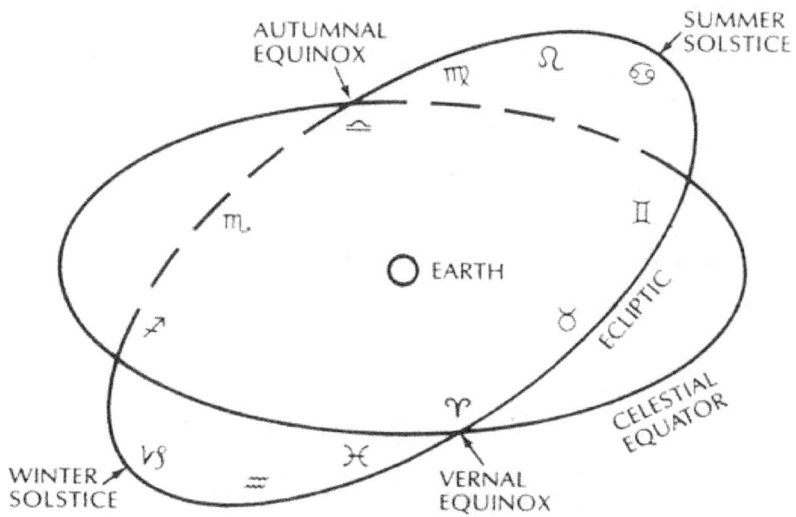

Figure 1 The Ecliptic

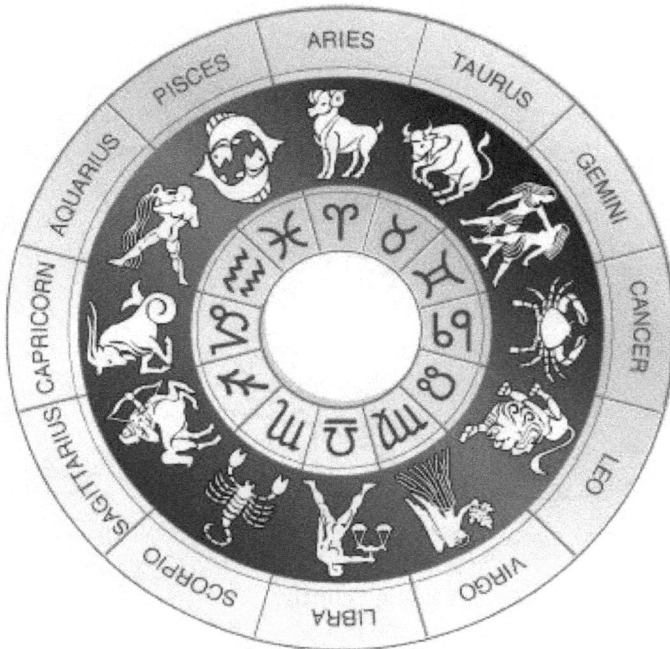

Figure 2 The Zodiac Wheel

If you have ever wondered about the names of the zodiac wheel portions, the following descriptions may be of interest. To ancient civilizations, each of these twelve signs was named after groupings and patterns of stars visible in the heavens to the high priests.

Aries (The Ram)

(0 to 30 degrees) 21 March – 20 April

According to Greek mythology, Nephele, the mother of Phrixus and Helle, gave her sons a ram with a golden fleece. To escape their evil stepmother, Hera, the sons mounted the ram and fled. When they reached the sea, Helles fell into the water and perished. Phrixus survived the ordeal and upon arriving in Colchis was received by King Aeetes who sacrificed the ram and dedicated the fleece to Zeus. Zeus then transported the ram into the heavens and made it into a constellation.

Taurus (The Bull)

(30 to 60 degrees) 21 April – 21 May

According to Roman legend, Jupiter took the form of a bull and became infatuated with the fair maiden Europa. When Europa decided to ride the bull, it rushed into the sea and whisked Europa off to Crete. Jupiter then raised the bull into the heavens where it became a star.

Gemini (The Twins)

(60 to 90 degrees) 22 May – 21 June

In Greek mythology, Hercules and Apollo are twins. In Roman legend, these twins are said to be Castor and Pollux, the sons of Leda. Pollux was the son of Zeus, who seduced Leda, while Castor was the son of Tyndareus, King of Sparta. Castor and Pollux are mythologically associated with St. Elmo's fire in their role as protectors of sailors. When Castor died, because he was mortal, Pollux begged Zeus to give Castor immortality. Zeus granted the wish by uniting Castor and Pollux together in the heavens as a constellation.

Cancer (The Crab)

(90 to 120 degrees) 22 June-23 July

Roman legend says that Cancer is the crab that bit Hercules during his fight with the Hydra monster. The crab was then placed in the heavens as a star by Juno, the enemy of Hercules.

Leo (The Lion)

(120 to 150 degrees) 24 July – 23 August

Legend says that Hercules battled with the Nemean lion and won. Zeus raised the lion to the heavens as a star.

Virgo (The Virgin)

(150 to 180 degrees) 24 August – 23 September

Legend has it that Virgo is a constellation modelled after Justitia, daughter of Astraeus and Ancora. Justitia lived before mankind sinned. After mankind sinned, Justitia returned to the heavens.

Libra (The Scales)

(180 to 210 degrees) 24 September – 23 October

Libra was known in Babylonian astronomy as a set of scales that were held sacred to the Sun God Shamash, the patron of truth and justice. In Roman mythology, Libra is considered to depict the scales held by Astraea , the Goddess of Justice.

Scorpio (The Scorpion)

(210 to 240 degrees) 24 October – 22 November

According to Greek mythology, Orion boasted to Diana and Latona that he could kill every animal on Earth. The ladies sent for a scorpion which stung Orion to death. Jupiter then raised the scorpion to the heavens as a constellation.

Sagittarius (The Archer)

(240 to 270 degrees) 23 November – 22 December

In Babylonian legend, Sagittarius was the God of War. In Greek legend, Sagittarius was a centaur (half man, half horse) in the act of shooting an arrow. In Roman legend, Sagittarius was a centaur who killed himself when he accidently dropped one of Hercules' poisoned arrows on his hoof.

Capricorn (The Goat)

(270 to 300 degrees) 23 December – 20 January

In Greek legend, during the war with the giants the Greek Gods were driven into Egypt. In order to escape the wrath of the encroaching giants, each Greek God changed his shape. The God Pan leapt into the river Nile and turned the upper part of his body into a goat and the lower part into a fish. This combination was deemed worthy by Jupiter who raised Pan to the heavens.

Aquarius (The Water Bearer)

(300 to 330 degrees) 21 January – 19 February

According to legend, Deucalion- the son of Prometheus, was raised to the heavens after surviving the great deluge that flooded the world.

Pisces (The Fishes)

(330 to 360 degrees) 20 February - 20 March

In Greek legend, Aphrodite and Eros were surprised by Typhon while playing along the river Nile. To escape, they jumped into the water and were changed into two fishes.

2. Financial Astrology

The Celestial Bodies

In addition to the Sun and Moon, there are eight celestial bodies important to the application of Astrology to trading and investing on the financial markets. These planets are Mercury, Venus, Mars, Jupiter, Saturn, Uranus, Neptune and Pluto.

The Glyphs

These planets and the twelve signs of the zodiac are denoted by strange looking symbols, called *glyphs*. Figure 3 presents the glyphs.

Points		Zodiac Signs	
☉	Sun	♈	Aries
☾	Moon	♉	Taurus
☿	Mercury	♊	Gemini
♀	Venus	♋	Cancer
♂	Mars	♌	Leo
♃	Jupiter	♍	Virgo
♄	Saturn	♎	Libra
♅	Uranus	♏	Scorpio
♆	Neptune	♐	Sagittarius
♇ ♇	Pluto	♑	Capricorn
		♒	Aquarius
		♓	Pisces

Figure 3 – The Glyphs

Ascendant, Descendant, MC and IC

As the Earth rotates on its axis once in every 24 hours, an observer situated on Earth will detect an apparent motion of the zodiac. To better define this motion, astrologers apply four cardinal points to the zodiac, almost like the north, south, east and west points on a compass. These cardinal points divide the zodiac into four quadrants. The east point is termed the *Ascendant* and is often abbreviated Asc. The west point is termed the *Descendant* and is often abbreviated Dsc. The south point is termed the *Mid-Heaven* (from the Latin *Medium Coeli*) and is often abbreviated MC. The north point is termed the *Imum Coeli* (Latin for bottom of the sky) and is abbreviated IC.

Geocentric and Heliocentric Astrology

Financial Astrology comes in two distinct varieties – *geocentric* and *heliocentric*.

In *geocentric* Astrology, the Earth is the vantage point for observing the planets as they pass through the signs of the zodiac. Owing to the different times for the planets to each orbit the Sun, an astrologer situated on Earth would see the planets making distinct angles (called *aspects*) with one another and also with the Sun. The aspects that are commonly used in Astrology are 0, 30, 45, 60, 90, 120, 150 and 180 degrees. In Financial Astrology, it is common to refer to only the 0, 45, 90, 120 and 180 degree aspects.

In *heliocentric* Astrology, the Sun is the vantage point for observing the planets as they pass through the signs of the zodiac. An observer positioned on the Sun would also see the orbiting planets making *aspects* with one another.

To identify these aspects, astrologers use Ephemeris Tables. For geocentric Astrology, the *New American Ephemeris for the 21ˢᵗ Century* is commonly used. It is available at most bookstores. For heliocentric Astrology, the *American Heliocentric Ephemeris* is a good resource. It tends to be harder to find in bookstores but on-line booksellers may have it available.

For faster aspect determination, two excellent software programs available are *Millenium Trax* produced by AIR Software and *Solar Fire Gold* produced by Astrolabe. My preference is the *Solar Fire Gold* product. I also use a market platform called Market Analyst. This brilliant piece of software, (originally developed in Australia) allows the user to generate an end of day price chart and then overlay various astrological aspects and occurrences onto the chart. In my humble opinion, all serious adherents of financial Astrology should spend the money to acquire this software program.

Lunar Astrology

On any clear night the Moon will be visible in one of its various phases. The Moon is the closest of all the planetary bodies to the Earth and has long been held in fascination by mankind.

Throughout the centuries, the Moon has been associated with health, mood and dreams. In 6th century Constantinople (modern day Istanbul, Turkey), physicians at the court of Emperor Justinian advised that gout could be cured by inscribing verses of Homer on a copper plate when the Moon was in the sign of Libra or Leo. In 17th century France, astrologers used the Moon to explain mood changes in women. In 17th century England, herbal remedy practitioners advised people to pluck the petals of the peony flower when the Moon was waning. During the Renaissance period, it was thought that dreams could come true if the Moon was in the signs of Taurus, Leo, Aquarius or Scorpio.

Today, such ideas about the Moon are no more. But, the Moon nonetheless continues to be recognized as a powerful celestial body. Just as the gravitational pull of the Moon can influence the action of ocean tides, this same pull somehow also influences our emotions of fear and hope. As our emotions of fear and hope change, our investment buying and selling decisions also change. These emotional changes correlate to changes in price trend action. When this correlation is overlaid with technical chart analysis, a whole new dimension in trading and investing opens up.

The Lunar Month

Just as the planets orbit 360 degrees around the Sun, the Moon orbits 360 degrees around the Earth. The Moon orbits the Earth in a plane of motion called the *lunar orbit plane*. This plane is inclined at about 5 degrees to the celestial equator plane of the Earth. The Moon orbits Earth with a slightly elliptical pattern in approximately 27.3 days, relative to an observer located on a fixed frame of reference such as the Sun. This time period is known as a *sidereal month*. However, during one sidereal month, an observer located on Earth (a moving frame of reference) will revolve part way around the Sun. To that Earth-bound observer, a complete orbit of the Moon around the Earth will appear longer than the sidereal month at approximately 29.5 days. This 29.5 day period of time is known as a *synodic month* or more commonly a *lunar month*.

Retrograde

Think of the planets orbiting the Sun as a group of race cars travelling around a racetrack. Consider what happens as a fast moving car approaches a slower moving car from behind. At first, all appears normal. An observer in the fast moving car sees the slower moving car heading in the same direction. Gradually, the observer in the fast car sees that he will soon overtake the slow car. For a brief moment in time as the fast car overtakes the slower car the observer in the fast car notices that the slower car appears to stand still. Of course the slow car is not really standing still. This is simply an optical illusion.

These brief illusory periods are what astrologers call Retrograde events. To ancient societies, Retrograde events were of great significance as human emotion was often seen to be changeable at these events.

There will be three or four times during a year when Earth and Mercury pass by each other on this celestial racetrack. There will be one or perhaps two times per year when Earth and Venus pass each other. There will be one time every two years when Earth and Mars pass each other.

Declination

Declination refers to the positioning of a celestial body above or below the Earth's celestial equator plane. Celestial bodies experience declinations of up to about 25 degrees above and below the celestial equator plane.

My market back-testing research has revealed that changes in the declination of a celestial body can affect the human psyche. Why this happens remains a mystery to me.

Moon, Mercury, Venus, Mars and indeed Earth itself endure frequent changes in declination due to the gravitational force of the Sun. Planets like Jupiter, Saturn, Neptune, Uranus and Pluto also experience declination changes but these changes are slow to evolve.

Elongation and Separation

The orbit of a planet around the Sun is not a perfectly circular event. Rather, planets orbit the Sun is elliptical paths. For example, Mercury orbits the Sun in about 88 days. There will be times in its elliptical orbit when it is far from the Sun and there will be times when it is close to the Sun. More specifically, the times when a planet is farthest from the Sun are called Perihelion events or Perigee events. Times when a planet is closest to the Sun are called Aphelion events or Apogee events.

This phenomenon applies to the Moon in its path around the Earth as well. Apogee events occur when the Moon is closest to Earth. Perigee events occur when Moon is farthest from Earth.

From an observers vantage point on Earth, there will also be times when planets are seen to be at maximum angles of separation from the Sun. These events are what astronomers refer to as maximum easterly and westerly elongations.

Conjunctions

Mercury and Venus are closer to the Sun than is the Earth. From our vantage point on Earth, there will be times when Mercury or Venus are between us and the Sun. Likewise, there will be times when the Sun is between us and Mercury or Venus. On the zodiac wheel, the times when Mercury or Venus are at the same zodiac sign and degree as the Earth are what astronomers call conjunctions.

An Inferior Conjunction occurs with Mercury or Venus between Earth and the Sun. A Superior Conjunction occurs with the Sun between Earth and Mercury or Venus.

Conjunction events are closely related to Retrograde events in that they occur on either side of Retrograde events. For example, in 2015 Venus was Retrograde from late July to early September. Its actual Inferior Conjunction was recorded on August 15. When Venus is at Inferior Conjunction, it is visible as a Morning Star. When it is at Superior Conjunction it is visible as an Evening Star.

3. Retrograde and Declination 2016

For 2016, Mercury will be Retrograde from:

January 6 through January 25

April 29 through May 22

August 31 through September 22

December 20 through January 9, 2017

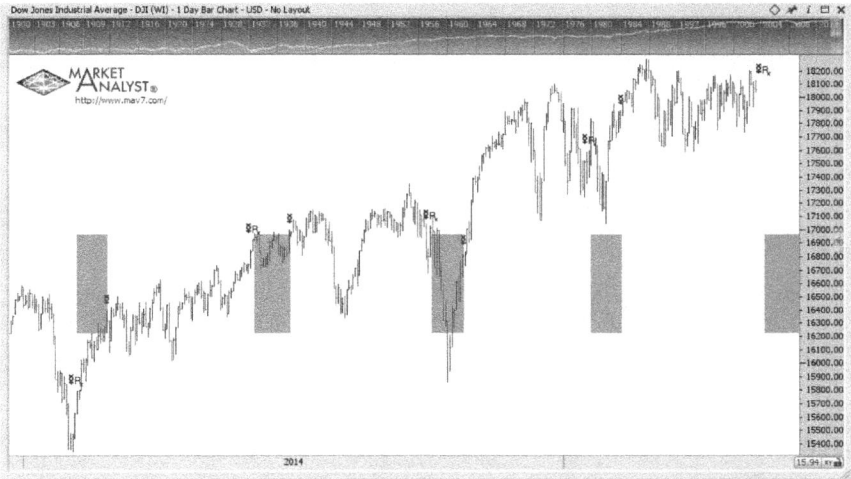

Figure 4 – Mercury Retrograde and the Dow Jones Average

To illustrate the use of Mercury Retrograde as a tool to assist one with trading or investing, consider the chart in Figure 4 above. This chart has been generated in the Market Analyst program. Mercury Retrograde events are illustrated by the dark shaded bars overlaid on the chart. Notice how all too often these bars align to sharp swings in trend.

For 2016, Venus will be not exhibit any Retrograde motion.

For 2016, Mars will be Retrograde from:

April 17 through June 29

Mars Retrograde does not affect all markets in a like manner. One market where Mars Retrograde events tend to deliver sharp volatility is the 10 Year Treasury Futures.

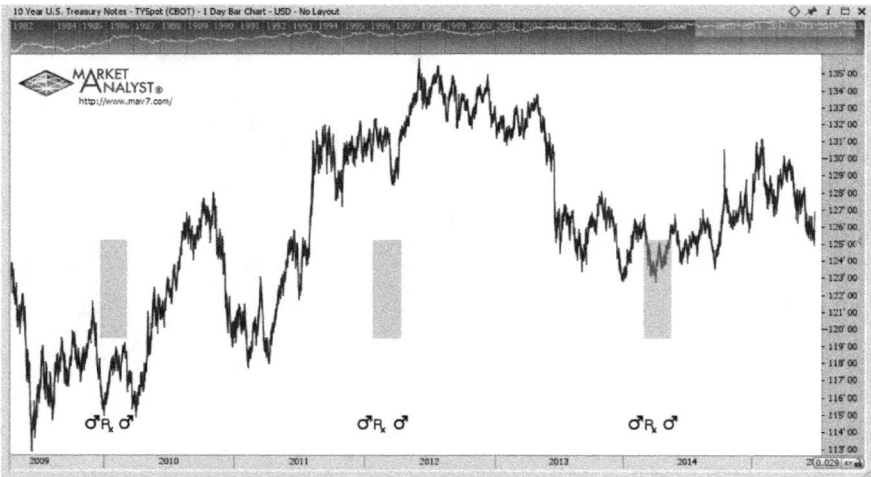

Figure 5 – Mars Retrograde and the 10 Year Treasury Note Futures

The 10 Year Treasuries are volatile enough to begin with. However, traders of these futures should be alert for sharp price swings and trend changes during Mars Retrograde events as Figure 5 illustrates.

In December 2015, Mercury will be at about 25 degrees southerly declination. From this low point, Mercury will begin to climb higher in declination.

Between January 7 and January 20, Mercury will make a brief inflection point in its declination path before continuing its upward climb.

Between April 19 and May 3, Mercury will again exhibit an inflection in its journey as it hits 22 degrees of declination.

After easing off to 15 degrees of declination, Mercury will again record an inflection point between May 20 and June 3.

Between June 27 and July 10, Mercury will be at its 2016 maximum declination of 24 degrees.

Mercury will then fall in declination. Between August 24 and September 6, Mercury will record an inflection point at 2 degrees southerly declination.

Between September 20 and October 3, Mercury will register another inflection at 5 degrees northerly declination.

Mercury will then steadily fall in declination and from late November to early December will record its lowest declination for 2016 at 26 degrees southerly declination.

Figure 6 illustrates the declination path for Mercury during 2016.

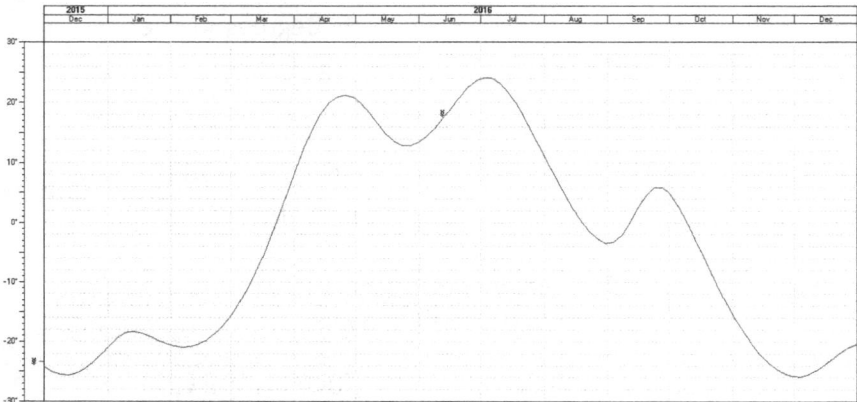

Figure 6 Mercury Declination

Between January 17 and February 6, Venus will make a low point in its declination at 22 degrees southerly before continuing its upward climb.

From June 12 to June 30, Venus will record its maximum declination for 2016 at 24 degrees northerly.

Venus will then steadily decline in declination and will record its 2016 low point between November 8 and November 24 at 26 degrees southerly.

Figure 7 illustrates the declination path for Venus during 2016.

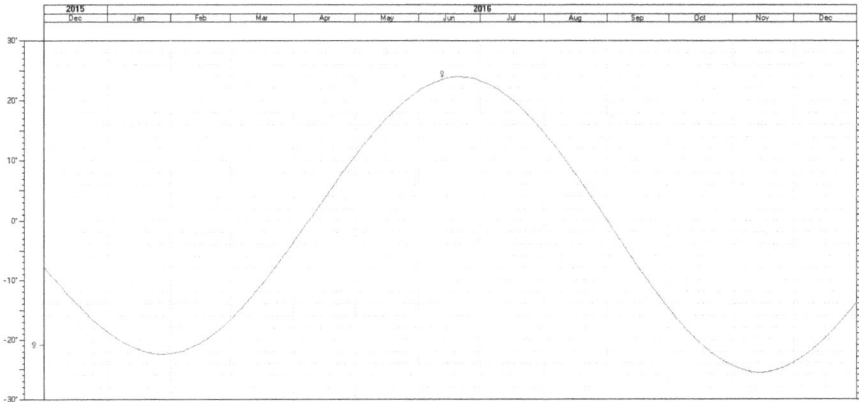

Figure 7 Venus Declination

Early January 2016 will see Mars at about 10 degrees southerly declination. Mars will slowly lose declination until recording its minimum at 26 degrees southerly in late September.

Figure 8 illustrates the declination path for Mars in 2016.

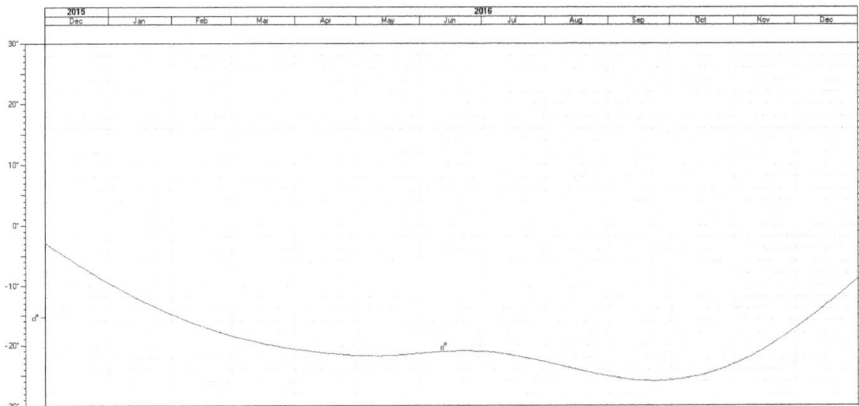

Figure 8 Mars Declination

Declination of Sun really does not ever change. What does change is how we on Earth view the Sun.

From March 18 to 23, the Sun from our viewpoint on Earth passes through 0 degrees of declination. This point in our calendar year has come to be called the Spring Equinox.

From June 3 to July 8, the Sun passes through its declination maximum for the year. This is what is commonly called the Summer Solstice.

From September 20 to 26, Sun passes through 0 degrees declination. This is what is commonly called the Autumn Equinox.

From December 9 to 30, Sun passes through its lowest declination level for the year. This is what is commonly referred to as the Winter Solstice.

Figure 9 illustrates the declination path for Sun in 2016.

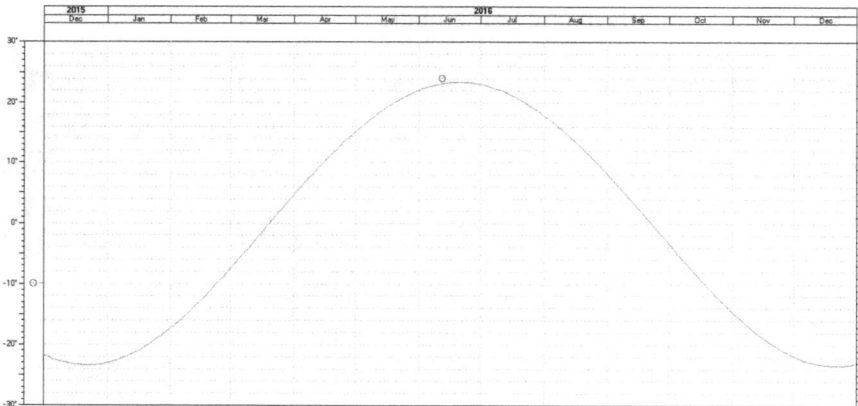

Figure 9 Sun Declination

During each lunar cycle, the Moon can be seen to vary in its position above and below the lunar ecliptic.

Figure 10 presents a plot of Moon declination for 2016.

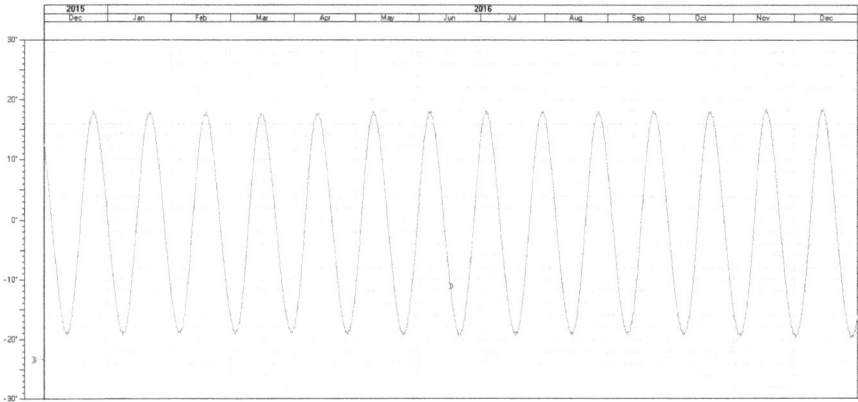

Figure 10 Moon Declination

Take a look at a daily chart of a stock you like to trade or invest in. Take a look at a commodity futures contract you follow. You will often find that at times of maximum or minimum lunar declination there will be a short term change in price behavior best witnessed on a 4 hour chart.

To assist you in some back-testing of your own, consider that in 2015, Moon recorded maximums in declination on January 3, January 31, February 27, March 26, April 22, May 20, June 16, July 14, August 10, September 7, October 4, November 1, November 28.

To further assist you, consider that in 2015, Moon recorded minimums in declination on January 18, February 15, March 14, April 10, May 7, June 4, July 1, July 29, August 25, September 21, October 19, November 15, December 12.

For 2016, Moon will record maximums in its declination on January 21, February 18, March 16, April 12, May 10, June 6, July 4, July 31, August 27, September 23, October 20, November 17 and December 15.

For 2016, Moon will record minimums in its declination on January 8, February 5, March 3, March 31, April 27, May 24, June 20, July 18, August 14, September 11, October 8, November 4, December 1 and December 29.

To illustrate the use of declination as a tool to help one navigate the financial markets consider the following chart in Figure 11 where Venus declination events have been overlaid onto a chart of the STOXX 50 Index from 2012 to mid-2015. Note the short term trend shifts as Venus approaches, records and then leaves its maximum declination. Similarly, note the like behavior at the minimum declination points. Declination should not be used as a pinpoint precision instrument. Rather, as a declination maximum or minimum event is unfolding, use your preferred chart technical momentum indicators to alert you to trend shifts.

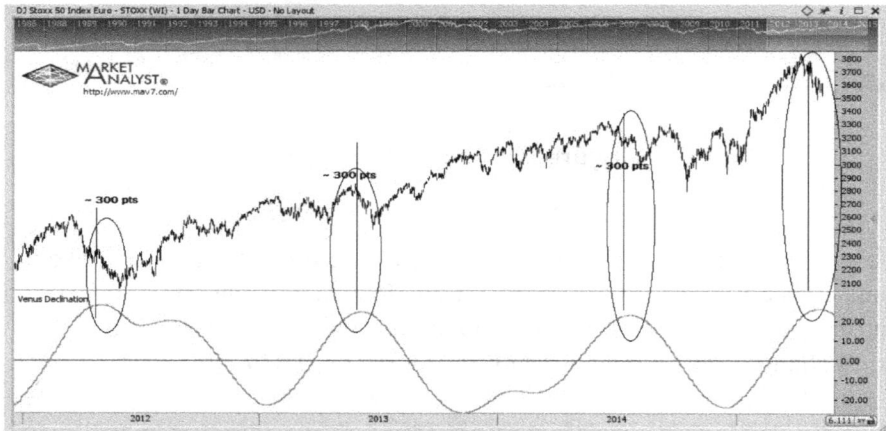

Figure 11 Venus Declination

4. Elongation, Conjunction and Separations 2016

During 2015, the Moon was at Apogee to the Earth on January 9, February 5, March 4, April 1, April 28, May 26, June 23, July 21, August 17, September 14, October 11, November 7 and December 5.

During 2015, Moon was at Perigee to the Earth on January 21, February 18, March 19, April 16, May 14, June 9, July 5, August 2, August 30, September 27, October 26, November 23 and December 21.

During 2016, Moon will be at Perigee on January 15, February 11, March 10, April 7, May 6, June 3, July 1, July 27, August 22, September 18, October 16, November 14 and December 12.

Moon in 2016 will be Apogee on January 30, February 27, March 25, April 21, May 18, June 15, July 13, August 10, September 6, October 4, October 31, November 7 and December 25.

Traders interested in using lunar apogee and perigee events to complement their trading actions should ideally be using something like a 4 hour chart along with one or more suitable technical indicators. To better illustrate apogee and perigee, consider the chart of the Dow Jones Average in Figure 12 that has been overlaid with apogee and perigee events. Note the short term volatile price swings that align to these apogee and perigee events.

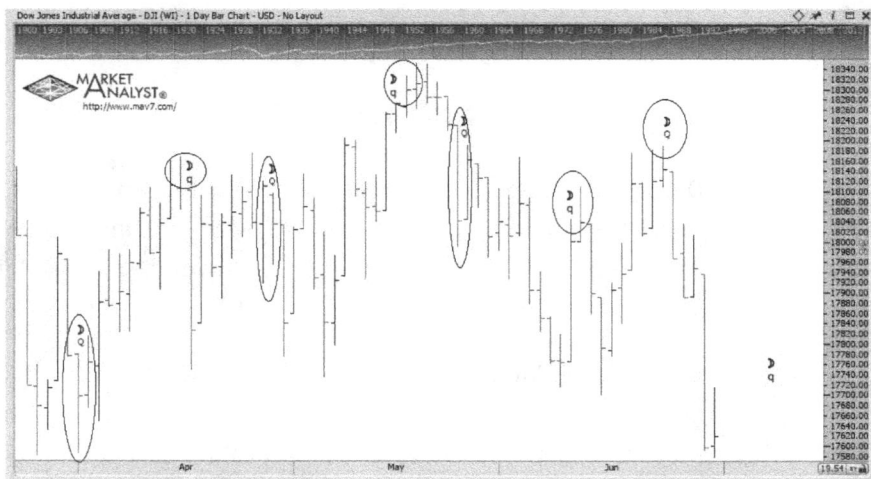

Figure 12 Moon Apogee and Perigee and the Dow Jones Average

During 2015, Mercury was at Perihelion on January 21, April 19, July 16 and October 12. During 2015, Mercury was at Aphelion on March 6, June 2, August 29 and November 25.

During 2016, Mercury will be at Perihelion on January 8, April 5, July 2, September 28 and December 25. Mercury will be at Aphelion on February 21, May 19, August 15 and November 11.

During 2015, Venus was at Perihelion on April 18 and at Aphelion on August 8.

During 2016, Venus will be at Perihelion on July 11 and at Aphelion on March 20.

During 2015, Mercury was at its maximum easterly elongation on January 14, May 7, September 4 and December 29. During 2015, Mercury was at its maximum westerly elongation on February 24, June 24 and October 16.

To better illustrate Mercury elongation as a potential tool to assist with trading decisions, consider the chart of the Dow Jones Average illustrated in Figure 13. This chart has been overlaid with Mercury points of maximum easterly and westerly elongation.

Figure 13   Mercury Elongation and the Dow Jones Average

For 2016, Mercury will be at its maximum easterly elongation on April 18, August 16 and again on December 11. Mercury will be at its maximum westerly elongations on February 7, June 5 and September 28.

During 2015, Venus was at its maximum easterly elongation on June 6 and at its maximum westerly elongation on October 26.

For 2016, there will be no Venus maximum elongation events. Venus will be at its greatest eastern elongation on January 12, 2017.

During 2015, Mercury was at Inferior Conjunction on January 30, May 30 and September 23. During 2015, Mercury was at Superior Conjunction at April 10, July 23 and November 17.

During 2016, Mercury will be at Inferior Conjunction on January 14, May 9, September 13 and December 28. Mercury will be at Superior Conjunction on March 23, July 7 and October 27.

Remember – the Mercury Inferior Conjunction events will always occur during a Mercury Retrograde event. While the Inferior conjunction event itself may not always align to a short term trend change, the retrograde event most likely will.

The last Venus Superior Conjunction event was October 25, 2014. Venus then entered Inferior Conjunction on August 15, 2015. It will enter Superior Conjunction again on June 6, 2016.

Whenever Venus records a Superior Conjunction event, it will shortly thereafter appear to the observer as an Evening Star. After recording an Inferior Conjunction, it will appear as a Morning Star.

Mercury will exhibit similar behavior, but owing to the closeness of Mercury to the Sun it is often difficult to see it as a Morning Star.

5. New York Stock Exchange

2016 Astrology

The Lunation and the New York Stock Exchange

A *lunation* is the astrological term for a New Moon. At a lunation, the Sun and Moon are separated by 0 degrees which means the Sun and Moon are together in the same sign of the zodiac. The correlation between the monthly lunation event and New York Stock Exchange price movements was first popularized in 1937 by trader Louise McWhirter. In her book, *Theory of Stock Market Forecasting*, she discussed how lunations making hard aspects to planets such as Mars, Jupiter, Saturn and Uranus were indicative of coming volatility on the New York Stock Exchange. She also paid close attention to Mars and Neptune - the two planets that *rule* the New York Stock Exchange. McWhirter said those times of a lunar month when the transiting Moon makes 0 degree aspects to Mars and Neptune should be watched carefully.

New York Stock Exchange – First Trade Chart

The New York Stock Exchange officially opened for business on May 17, 1792. As the following horoscope shows, the NYSE has its Ascendant (Asc) at 14 degrees Cancer and its Mid-Heaven (MC) at 24 Pisces.

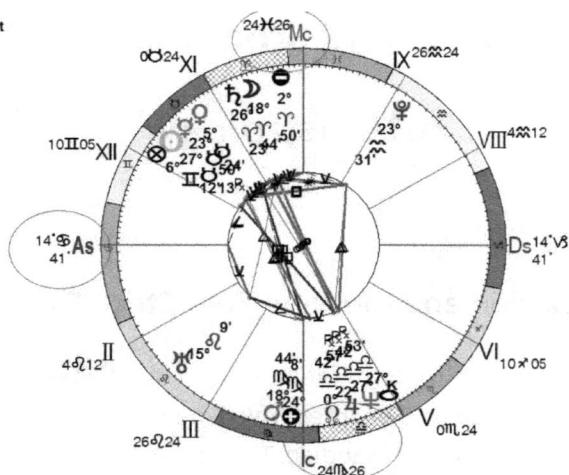

Figure 14: NYSE First Trade horoscope

McWhirter further paid close attention to those times in the monthly lunar cycle when the transiting Moon passed by the NYSE natal Asc and MC locations at 14 Cancer and 24 Pisces respectively.

Horoscope Charts and the McWhirter Methodology

In my research and writing, I follow the McWhirter methodology. When forecasting whether or not a coming month will be volatile or not for the NYSE, the McWhirter methodology starts with creating a horoscope chart for the New Moon date and positioning the Ascendant of the chart at 14 degrees Cancer - which is the Ascendant position on the 1792 natal chart of the New York Stock Exchange. Aspects to the lunation are then studied and planets that happen to be in the 10th House are also noted.

Similarly, when studying an individual stock or an individual commodity futures contract, the McWhirter approach calls for the creation of a horoscope chart at the First Trade date of the stock or commodity. The Ascendant is then shifted so that the Sun is at the Ascendant.

In stock and commodity analyses, McWhirter then paid strict attention to those times of a calendar year when transiting Sun, Mars, Jupiter, Saturn,

Neptune and Uranus made hard 0,90 and 180 degree aspects to the natal Mid-Heaven, natal Ascendant, natal Sun, natal Jupiter and even the natal Moon of the individual stock or commodity future being studied.

What one must be alert for at these hard aspects is the possibility of a trend change, the possibility of increased volatility within a trend or even the possibility of a breakout from a chart consolidation pattern. Evidence of such trend changes will be found by watching price action relative to moving averages and by utilizing oscillator type functions (MAC-D, DMI, RSI and so on). My personal experience says that the DMI and Wilder Volatility Stop are two excellent indicators to use. This Almanac assumes that the reader is reasonably well versed in chart technical analysis and the use of such indicators.

McWhirter Lunation Examples

The following three examples of the McWhirter method are taken from calendar year 2015.

January 2015

The New Moon in January 2015 occurred on January 20 at 0 degrees Aquarius. The horoscope wheel in Figure 15 depicts planetary placements just prior to the New Moon with the Ascendant at 14 Cancer - the same location it was at in 1792 when the New York Stock exchange was formed.

Event of 20 Jan 2015
Event Chart
20 Jan 2015, Tue
4:33:12 pm EDT +4:00
New York, NY
40°N42'51" 074°W00'23"
Geocentric
Tropical
Placidus
Mean Node
Parallax Moon

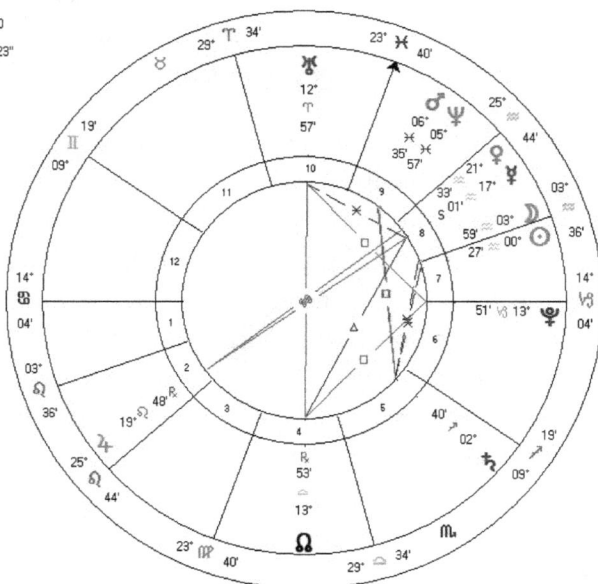

Figure 15 Lunation Event of January 20, 2015

The two co-rulers of the NYSE, Mars and Neptune, can be seen situated together at the 5 degree of Pisces location. However, the lunation itself makes no hard aspects to these planets. Nor does the lunation make any hard aspects to other planets. This suggests that the lunar cycle from January 20 to February 18, 2015 should generally be a positive one.

In fact this lunar cycle was a positive one with the Dow Jones Average gaining 500 points. However, this lunar cycle was not without extreme volatility. It is interesting to note how the transits of the Moon past the Mid Heaven (24 Pisces) and the Ascendant (14 Cancer) marked significant inflection points on the Dow Jones Average. The transit of Moon past the Mid-Heaven was preceded one day earlier by its transit of Mars and Neptune, the two co-rulers. The price chart in Figure 16 illustrates further.

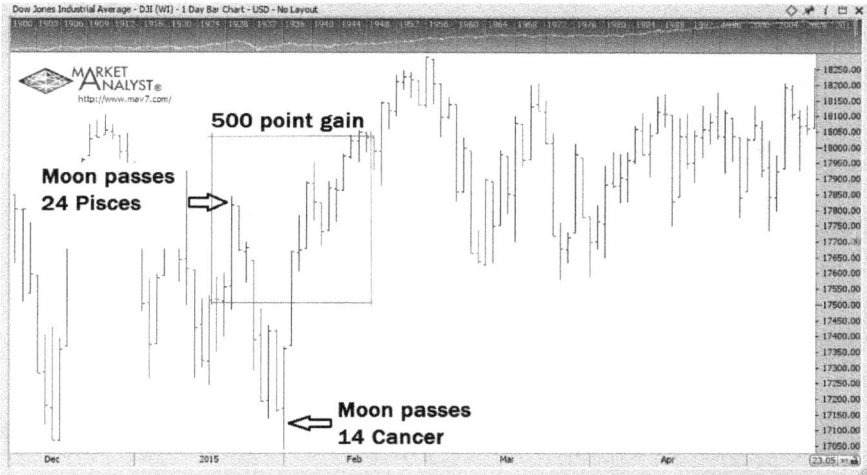

Figure 16 The January 2015 lunar cycle

February 2015

The next New Moon in 2015 occurred on February 18 at 29 degrees Aquarius. The horoscope wheel in Figure 17 depicts planetary placements just prior to the New Moon with the Ascendant at 14 Cancer.

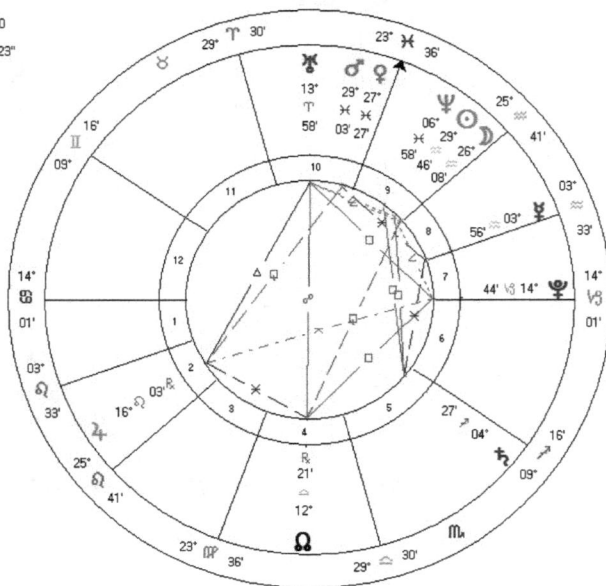

Figure 17 Lunation Event of February 18, 2015

Note that the lunation makes a hard 90 degree aspect to heavy-weight planet Saturn. As well, the lunation is within orb of being conjunct to co-ruler Neptune. These aspects are highly suggestive of a challenging lunar cycle for the Dow Jones Average.

In fact, it was a challenging lunar cycle with the Dow Jones only recording a net gain of 100 points. The price chart in Figure 18 illustrates further. Note the peak and subsequent trend change as Moon passed the 14 of Cancer point. Note the added price weakness in early March as aggressive planet Mars made a hard 90 degree aspect to the 14 of Cancer natal Ascendant point. Note the sharp gain of 225 points in mid-March as Moon passed co-ruler Neptune. This date also happened to be a US Federal Reserve meeting date. Traders and investors are advised to be very alert when these FOMC meeting dates fall on the same date as a transit of Moon past a key astrological point in the NYSE natal chart.

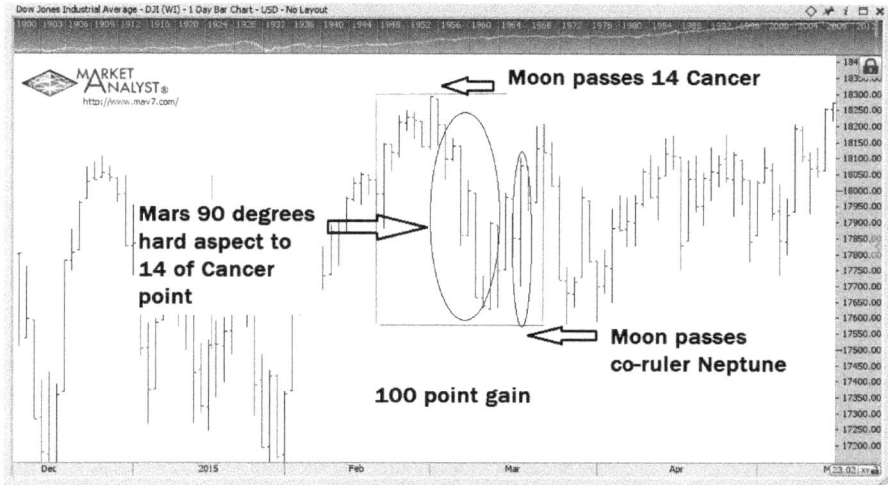

Figure 18 The February 2015 Lunar Cycle

May 2015

The New Moon in May 2015 occurred on May 17 at 26 degrees Taurus. The horoscope wheel in Figure 19 depicts planetary placements just prior to the New Moon with the Ascendant at 14 Cancer.

Note that this lunation was conjunct to co-ruler Mars. The lunation was also 180 degrees hard aspect to heavy-weight planet Saturn. In my 2015 Almanac for this lunation I expressly cautioned to be alert for a trend change on the Dow Jones Average.

In fact, the Dow Jones did record a trend change and went on to record a net loss of 400 points for this lunar cycle which ended June 16. Figure 20 illustrates the price action in more detail. The trend change occurred with Moon passing co-ruler Mars and also 14 of Cancer. A swing upwards then started with Moon passing co-ruler Neptune and also the 24 Pisces point.

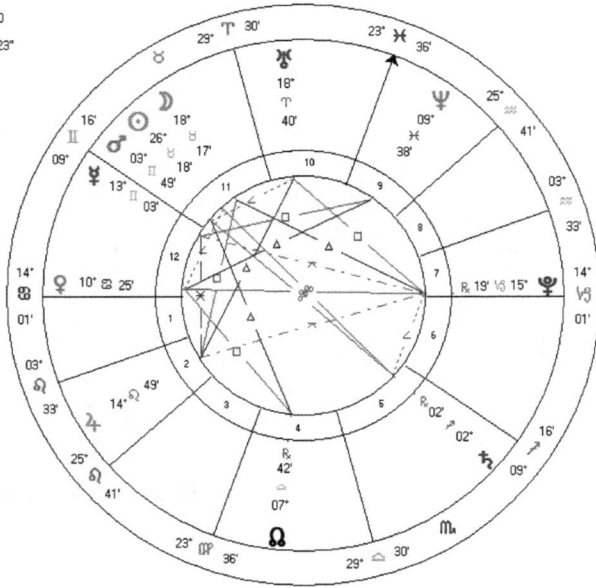

Figure 19 Lunation Event of May 17, 2015

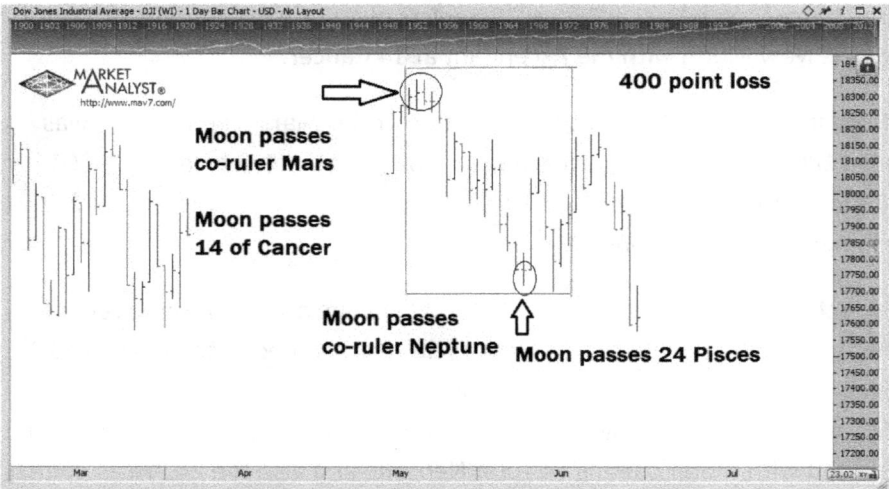

Figure 20 The May 2015 Lunation Cycle

2016 Lunation Forecasts

December 2015

Key Dates

The New Moon in December 2015 occurs on the 11th with Sun at 18 degrees Sagittarius. The horoscope in Figure 21 depicts planetary placements just hours prior to the New Moon with the Ascendant at 14 of Cancer.

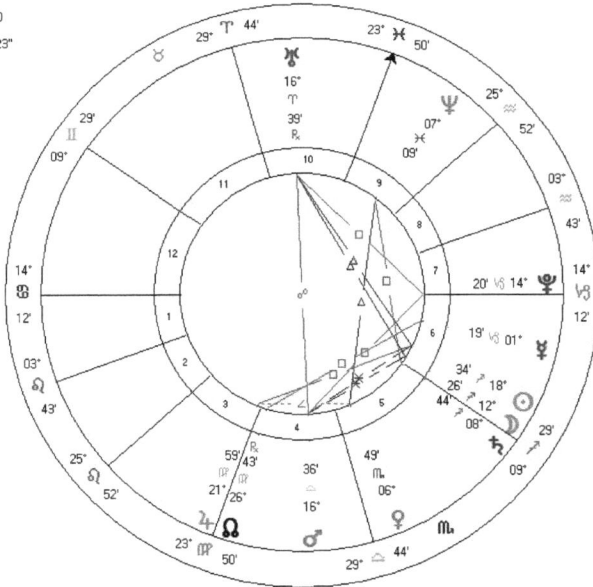

Figure 21 – New Moon December 11, 2015

The lunar cycle commencing at this New Moon will run until January 9, 2016. Although the lunation is close to Saturn and close to making a hard 90 degree aspect to co-ruler Neptune, there are no actual aspects evident. This is a positive indication for the coming lunar cycle.

Key dates to be alert to during this cycle include:

December 24: Moon transits past Mars. Watch for a reaction on what will be a shortened trading day ahead of the Holiday Season.

December 26: Moon transits past Neptune. The NYSE will most likely be closed so this transit matters not.

December 27: Moon transits past 24 Pisces (natal MC of NYSE). This date is a Saturday, so watch for a reaction on financial markets on the following Monday.

January 4: Moon transits past 14 Cancer (natal Asc of NYSE). This date is a Sunday, so watch for a reaction on the financial markets the next day, Monday.

January 5-14: Mars transits through 90 degrees to the NYSE natal Sun

January 2016

Key Dates

The New Moon in January occurs on the 9th with Sun at 19 degrees Capricorn. The horoscope in Figure 22 depicts planetary placements just hours prior to the New Moon as the Ascendant passes 14 Cancer.

The lunar cycle commencing at this New Moon will run until February 8, 2016. This lunation displays no hard aspects to any planets. This lunar cycle should in theory be generally favorable for the NYSE. However, traders and investors should remain cognizant that Mercury will be Retrograde at the time of this lunation which infers increased volatility. Also, Venus will be emerging from a low point in its declination path which infers a trend change.

Starting January 29 and continuing to February 14, Sun will be 90 degrees hard aspect to Mars . This infers increased volatility.

Event of 9 Jan 2016
Event Chart
9 Jan 2016, Sat
5:17:06 pm EDT +4:00
New York, NY
40°N42'51" 074°W00'23"
Geocentric
Tropical
Placidus
Mean Node
Parallax Moon

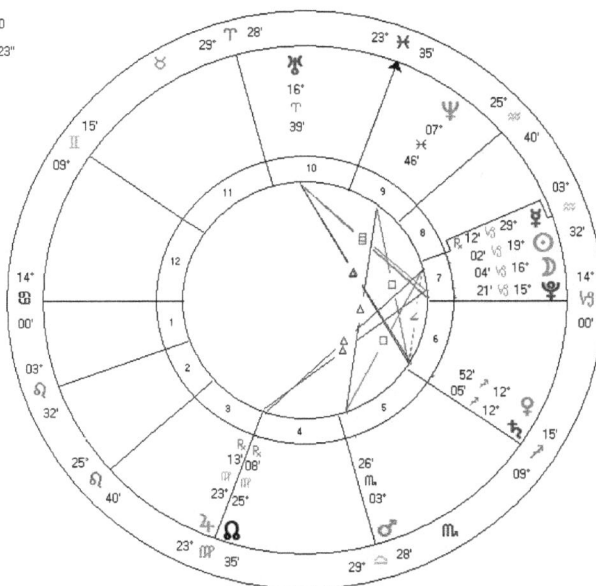

Figure 22 – New Moon January 9, 2016

Key dates to be alert to during this lunar cycle include:

January 12-13: Moon transits past co-ruler Neptune.

January 14: Moon transits past the NYSE natal Mid Heaven at 24 Pisces.

January 22:Moon transits 14 Cancer , the natal Asc position of the New York Stock Exchange.

The Federal Reserve FOMC meeting is slated for January 26-27. There are no astrological occurrences that align to this meeting.

February 1: Moon will complete its transit past co-ruler Mars.

February 2016

Key Dates

The New Moon in February occurs on the 8th with Sun at 19 degrees Aquarius. The following horoscope in Figure 23 depicts planetary placements just hours after the New Moon as the Ascendant passes 14 Cancer.

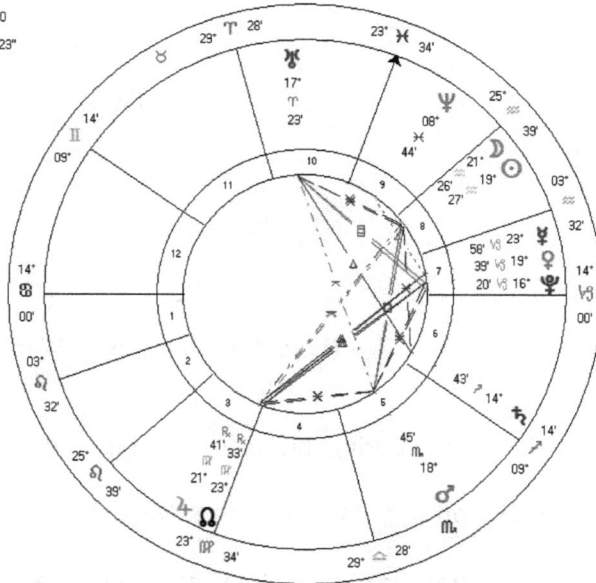

Figure 23 – New Moon February 8, 2016

The lunar cycle commencing at this New Moon will run until March 8, 2016. This lunation is interesting in that it makes a hard 90 degree aspect to NYSE co-ruler Mars. Traders and investors should also be cognizant that Mercury will be at its maximum westerly elongation on February 7. This lunar cycle could be a challenging one on the NYSE.

From February 28 through March 10, Sun will make a hard 90 degree aspect to Saturn. This infers a high potential for increased volatility.

Key dates to be alert to during this lunation include:

February 9-10: Moon transits past NYSE co-ruler Neptune.

February 11: Moon transits past the natal Mid-Heaven point of 24 Pisces.

February 18-19: Moon transits past the natal Ascendant point of 14 Cancer.

February 29: Moon transits past NYSE co-ruler Mars.

March 8: Moon transits past NYSE co-ruler Neptune mere hours before the New Moon event.

March 2016

Key Dates

The New Moon in March occurs on the 8th with Sun at 18 degrees Pisces. The following horoscope in Figure 24 depicts planetary placements just hours prior to the New Moon as the Ascendant passes 14 Cancer.

The lunar cycle commencing at this New Moon will run until April 7, 2016. This lunation is a complex one. It is 180 degrees hard aspect in opposition to expansive planet Jupiter which implies not all of Jupiter's beneficial energy will be felt. The lunation is also a hard aspect 90 degrees to Saturn. Saturn in turn is a hard 90 degrees to Jupiter.

Watch for increased volatility on the NYSE in what could be another challenging month.

Event of 8 Mar 2016
Event Chart
8 Mar 2016, Tue
1:26:06 pm EDT +4:00
New York, NY
40°N42'51" 074°W00'23"
Geocentric
Tropical
Placidus
Mean Node
Parallax Moon

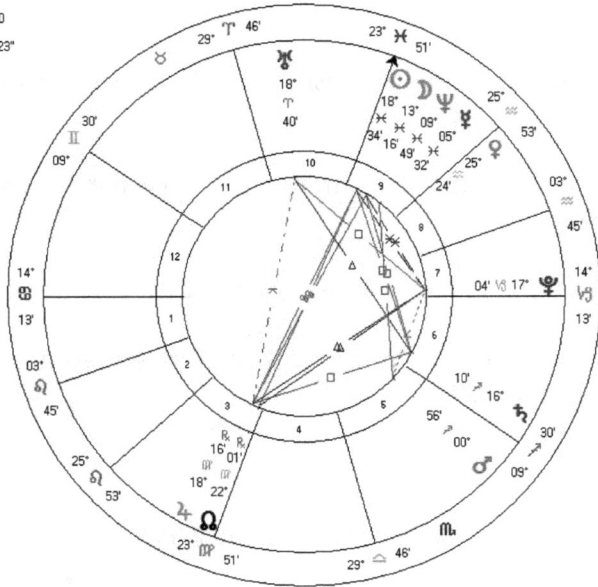

Figure 24 – New Moon March 8, 2016

Key dates to be alert to during this lunation include:

March 9: Moon transits past the NYSE natal Mid heaven point of 24 Pisces. This occurs just as a total solar eclipse takes place. This eclipse will be primarily visible to participants in Asian markets. Should Asian markets be adversely affected, watch for a carryover to North American markets.

The Federal Reserve FOMC meeting is slated for March 15-16 with a press conference to follow.

March 16: Moon transits past 14 Cancer, the natal Asc of the NYSE. This transit has implications for increased volatility especially with its alignment to the FOMC meeting.

Sun will be at a 120 degree trine aspect to Mars from March 21 through March 30. Such trine aspects are generally regarded as positive.

March 28: Moon transits past NYSE co-ruler Mars.

April 4: Moon transits past NYSE co-ruler Neptune.

April 2016

Key Dates

The New Moon in April occurs on the 7th with Sun at 18 degrees Aries. The horoscope in Figure 25 depicts planetary placements just hours after the New Moon as the Ascendant passes 14 Cancer.

The lunar cycle commencing at this New Moon will run until May 6, 2016. The lunation occurs in the 10th House in conjunction to heavy-weight planet Uranus. This is suggestive of added volatility. The lunation is also 120 degrees trine to heavyweight planet Saturn which is also suggestive of added volatility.

Venus crosses through 0 degrees of declination just as this lunation takes place. Such Venus declination events have a good potential to align to short term trend changes.

What may serve to offset any increased volatility towards month-end is Sun being 120 degrees trine to Jupiter from April 30 through May 6.

The Federal Reserve FOMC meeting is slated for April 26-27.

Event of 7 Apr 2016
Event Chart
7 Apr 2016, Thu
11:28:06 am EDT +4:00
New York, NY
40°N42'51" 074°W00'23"
Geocentric
Tropical
Placidus
Mean Node
Parallax Moon

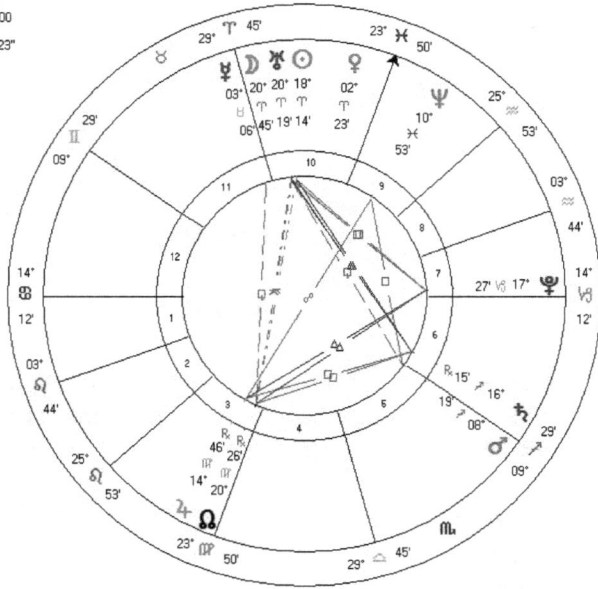

Figure 25 – New Moon April 7, 2016

Key dates to be alert to during this lunation include:

April 13: Moon transits past the natal Ascendant position of 14 Cancer.

April 25: Moon transits past NYSE co-ruler Mars.

May 2-3: Moon transits past NYSE co-ruler Neptune and also the natal Mid-Heaven point of 24 Pisces.

May 2016

Key Dates

The New Moon in May occurs on the 6th with Sun at 16 degrees Taurus. The horoscope in Figure 26 depicts planetary placements several hours prior to the New Moon as the Ascendant passes 14 Cancer.

The lunar cycle commencing at this New Moon will run until June 5, 2016. The lunation is a favorable 120 degree trine to expansive planet Jupiter. The lunation is also a favorable 60 degrees to co-ruler Neptune.

Traders and investors should further note that Mercury will be Retrograde at this lunation and also at its maximum easterly elongation.

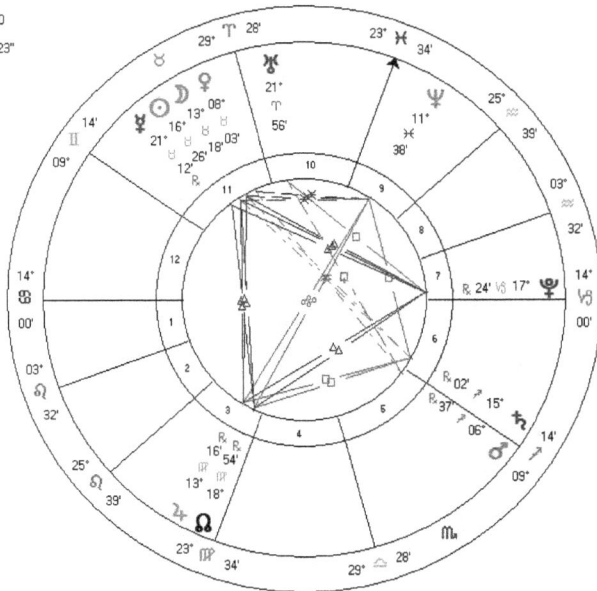

Figure 26 – New Moon May 6, 2016

Key dates to be alert to during this lunation include:

May 10: Moon transits past the natal Ascendant point of 14 Cancer.

May 21-22: Moon completes its transit past NYSE co-ruler Mars. This is a week-end. Watch for a market reaction on the Friday or the Monday.

May 29: Moon transits past co-ruler Neptune. This is a Sunday. Watch for a market reaction on the Monday.

May 30: Moon transits past 24 Pisces, the natal Mid-Heaven point of the NYSE

Sun will be at a 90 degree hard aspect to Jupiter from May 30 through June 8. Such hard aspects can lead to short term volatility swings.

June 2016

Key Dates

The New Moon in June occurs on the 5th with Sun at 15 degrees Gemini. The following horoscope in Figure 27 depicts planetary placements several hours after the New Moon as the Ascendant passes 14 Cancer.

The lunar cycle commencing at this New Moon will run until July 4, 2016.

This lunation carves out a peculiar Grand Cross pattern. The lunation is 90 degrees hard aspect to NYSE co-ruler Neptune, 90 degrees hard aspect to otherwise favorable planet Jupiter and 180 degrees opposite to Saturn.

Traders and investors should also remain cognizant that this lunation occurs just as Mercury is at its maximum westerly elongation.

In addition, this lunation takes place as both Venus and Sun are nearing their maximum declination points.

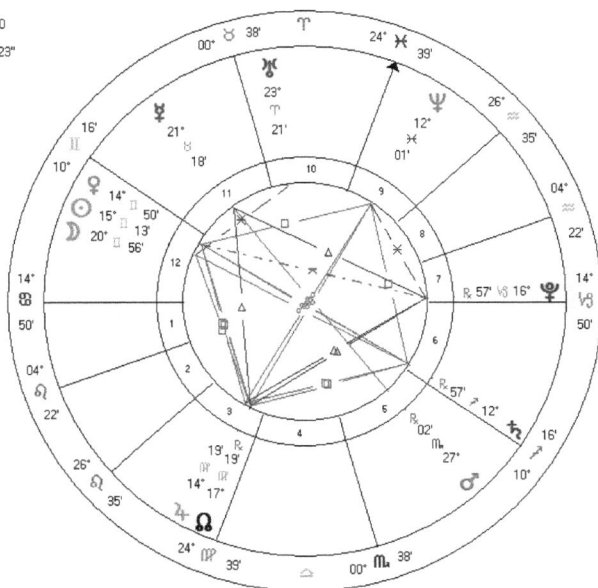

Event of 5 Jun 2016
Event Chart
5 Jun 2016, Sun
7:39:06 am EDT +4:00
New York, NY
40°N42'51" 074°W00'23"
Geocentric
Tropical
Placidus
Mean Node
Parallax Moon

Figure 27 – New Moon June 5, 2016

Key dates to be alert to during this lunation include:

June 6-7: Moon transits past the NYSE natal Ascendant point of 14 Cancer.

June 17: Moon transits NYSE co-ruler Mars.

June 25-27: Sun transits past NYSE co-ruler Neptune and also the NYSE natal Mid-Heaven point of 24 Pisces.

Traders and investors should remain cognizant that on June 14-15 the FOMC Committee will meet and the meeting will be followed by Federal Reserve Governor Janet Yellen hosting a press conference. While there are no specific lunar transits on these dates, one must (as noted above) remain vigilant as Venus and Sun will both be very nearly at their respective maximum declinations at this time.

This lunar cycle could prove to be highly interesting. A Grand Cross formation, a Mercury maximum elongation and Venus and Sun maximum declination events could deliver some extraordinary volatility.

July 2015

Key Dates

The New Moon in July occurs on the 4th with Sun at 12 degrees Cancer. The horoscope in Figure 28 depicts planetary placements at the New Moon as the Ascendant passes 14 Cancer.

The lunar cycle commencing at this New Moon will run until August 2, 2016.

This lunation is conjunct the always powerful 14 of Cancer point. It is furthermore a favorable 120 degrees trine to NYSE co-ruler Neptune.

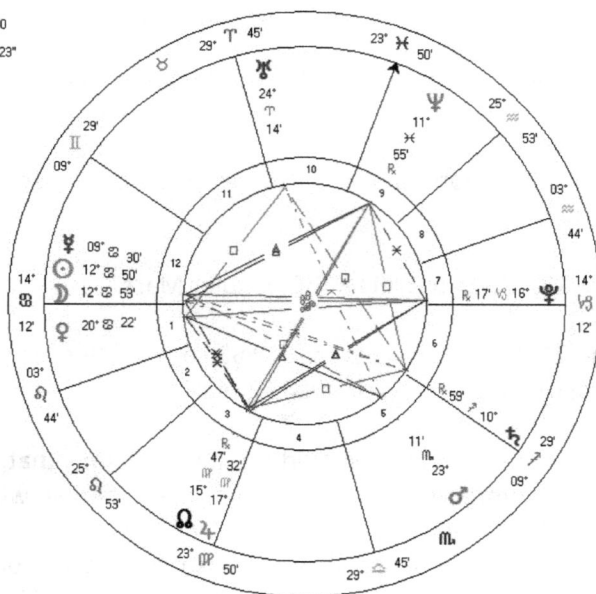

Figure 28 – New Moon July 4, 2016

Key dates to be alert to during this lunation include:

July 15: Moon completes its transit of NYSE co-ruler Mars.

July 23-24: Moon completes its transit of NYSE co-ruler Neptune and also its transit of the NYSE natal Mid-Heaven point of 24 Pisces. These transits occur on a Saturday-Sunday. Watch for a market reaction on the Friday or on the following Monday.

The Federal Reserve FOMC meeting is slated for July 26-27.

With this lunation occurring at the always powerful 14 of Cancer location, expect greater than usual volatility on the NYSE.

August 2016

Key Dates

The New Moon in August occurs on the 2nd with Sun at 10 degrees Leo. The horoscope in Figure 29 depicts planetary placements several hours prior to the New Moon as the Ascendant passes 14 Cancer.

The lunation can be seen to be 120 degrees trine to heavy-weight planet Saturn. There are no other visible aspects to this lunation. This set-up should be considered modest and the overall trend in place at the start of this lunation will likely continue.

The lunar cycle commencing at this New Moon will run until September 1, 2016.

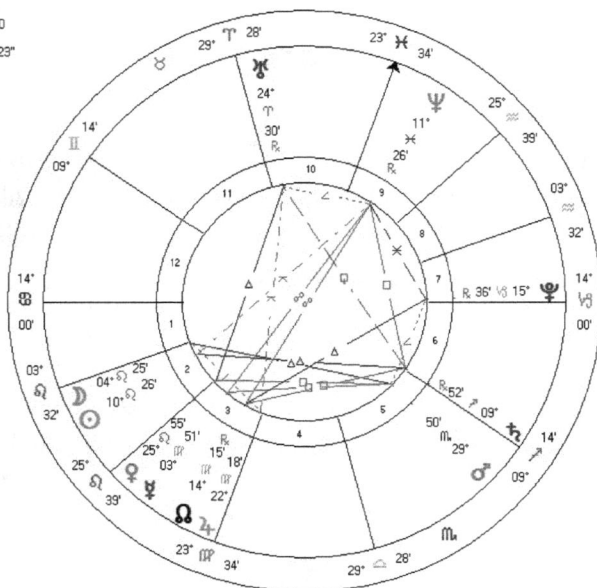

Event of 2 Aug 2016
Event Chart
2 Aug 2016, Tue
3:47:06 am EDT +4:00
New York, NY
40°N42'51" 074°W00'23"
Geocentric
Tropical
Placidus
Mean Node
Parallax Moon

Figure 29 – New Moon August 2, 2016

Key dates to be alert to during this lunation include:

August 12: Moon will transit past NYSE co-ruler Mars.

August 19-20: Moon transits past NYSE co-ruler Neptune and also past the NYSE natal Mid-Heaven point of 24 Pisces.

August 28: Moon transits past NYSE natal Ascendant point of 14 degrees Cancer. This date is Sunday. Watch for a market reaction either on the Friday beforehand or on the Monday immediately after this transit. This date also marks the onset of a hard 90 degree aspect between Sun and Saturn which will continue through to September 7.

September 2016

Key Dates

The New Moon in September occurs on the 1st with Sun at 9 degrees Virgo. The horoscope in Figure 30 depicts planetary placements several hours prior to the New Moon as the Ascendant passes 14 Cancer.

This lunation appears to be a charged one. It is 180 degrees hard aspect opposite to NYSE co-ruler Neptune. It is within orb of being 90 hard aspect square to Saturn and also to NYSE co-ruler Mars. In addition, just as this lunation occurs, Mercury will be turning Retrograde. Traders and investors should be alert for significant volatility on the NYSE.

The lunar cycle commencing at this New Moon will run until September 30, 2016.

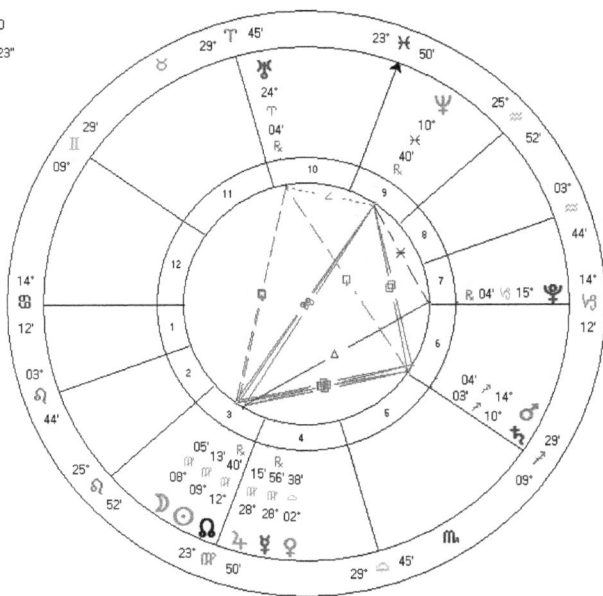

Figure 30 – New Moon September 1, 2016

Key dates to be alert to during this lunation include:

Venus will cross through 0 degrees of declination as the month of September gets underway. Watch for an increase in volatility.

September 4 through the 21st will feature Sun making a hard 90 degree aspect to aggressive planet Mars. This will contribute to any volatility.

September 9: Moon transits past NYSE co-ruler Mars.

September 15-16: Moon transits past NYSE co-ruler Neptune and also past the NYSE natal Mid-Heaven position of 24 Pisces.

September 17 through October 2 will feature Sun making a 0 degree conjunction to Jupiter. Such astro events all too often can align to trend changes.

Traders and investors should remain cognizant that on September 20-21, the FOMC Committee will meet and the meeting will be followed by Federal Reserve Governor Janet Yellen hosting a press conference. Curiously enough, this meeting comes just as Mercury Retrograde is completing itself. All too often I have noted significant trend changes at the end of a Mercury retrograde event.

September 24: Moon transits past the NYSE natal Ascendant location of 14 Cancer. This date is a Saturday. Watch for a possible market reaction on the Friday or even the following Monday. Immediately prior to this transit, Mercury retrograde concludes. All too often the conclusion of Mercury Retrograde events aligns to a sharp move on the market.

September 20-29: Transiting Sun will be 0 degrees conjunct to transiting Jupiter. Such conjunctions all too often align to significant inflection points on the market.

.

October 2016

Key Dates

The New Moon in October occurs on September 30th with Sun at 8 degrees Libra. The horoscope in Figure 31 depicts planetary placements several hours after the New Moon as the Ascendant passes 14 Cancer.

The lunation is within orb of being conjunct expansive planet Jupiter. This set-up bodes well for a positive lunar cycle.

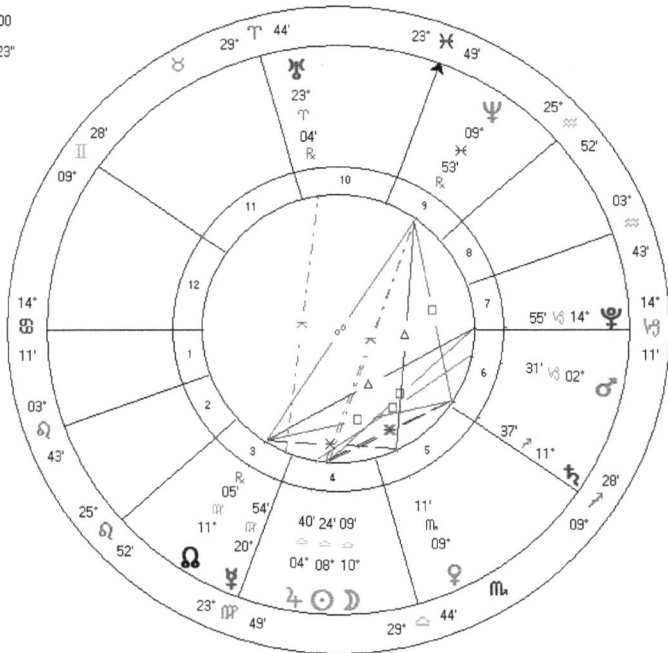

Figure 31 – New Moon September 30, 2016

The lunar cycle commencing at this New Moon will run until October 30, 2016.

Key dates to be alert to during this lunation include:

Mars will record its low point in declination as September wraps up and October gets underway. Watch for an associated increase in volatility.

October 7:Moon begins its transit past the NYSE co-ruler Mars.

October 12-14: Moon transits past NYSE co-ruler Neptune and also the NYSE natal Mid-Heaven point of 24 Pisces.

October 21: Moon transits past the NYSE natal Ascendant point of 14 Cancer.

November 2016

Key Dates

The New Moon cycle for November starts on the 30th of October with Sun at 8 degrees Scorpio. The horoscope in Figure 32 depicts planetary placements several hours after the New Moon as the Ascendant passes 14 Cancer.

The lunation is 120 degrees trine to NYSE co-ruler Neptune. This could have implications for a trend change or a marked increase in volatility on the NYSE.

The lunar cycle commencing at this New Moon will run until November 29, 2015.

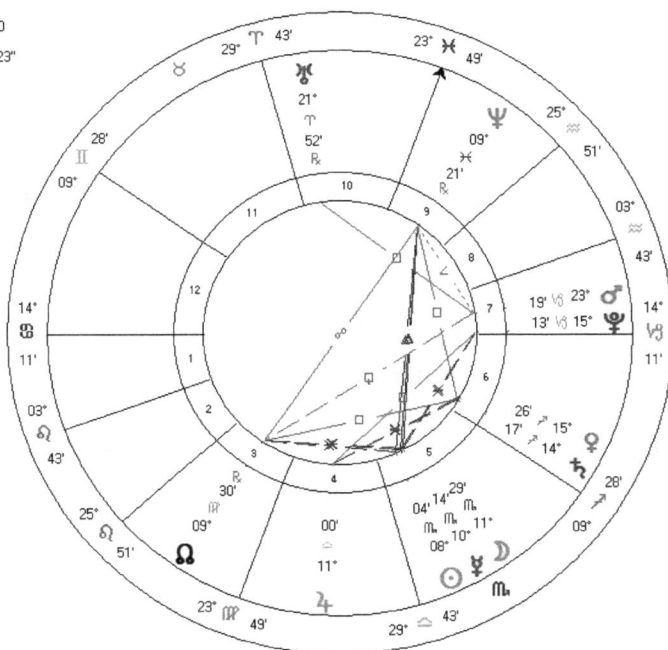

Event of 30 Oct 2016
Event Chart
30 Oct 2016, Sun
9:54:06 pm EDT +4:00
New York, NY
40°N42'51" 074°W00'23"
Geocentric
Tropical
Placidus
Mean Node
Parallax Moon

Figure 32 – New Moon October 30, 2016

Key dates to be alert to during this lunation include:

Traders and investors should remain cognizant that on November 1-2, the FOMC will meet. No press conference is slated for this meeting.

November 5: Moon transits past NYSE co-ruler Mars.

November 9-10: Moon transits past NYSE co-ruler Neptune as well as past the NYSE natal Mid-Heaven point of 24 Pisces. These transits occur one day after the USA Presidential Election.

Venus will carve out its declination minimum starting at this point in November. Watch for an associated trend change.

November 17: Moon transits past the NYSE natal Ascendant point of 14 Cancer.

December 2016

Key Dates

The New Moon cycle for December starts on the 29th of November with Sun at 7 degrees Sagittarius. The horoscope in Figure 33 depicts planetary placements several hours prior to the New Moon as the Ascendant passes 14 Cancer.

The lunation is 90 degrees hard aspect square to Neptune. This implies more than normal volatility for the NYSE.

The lunar cycle commencing at this New Moon will run until December 28, 2016.

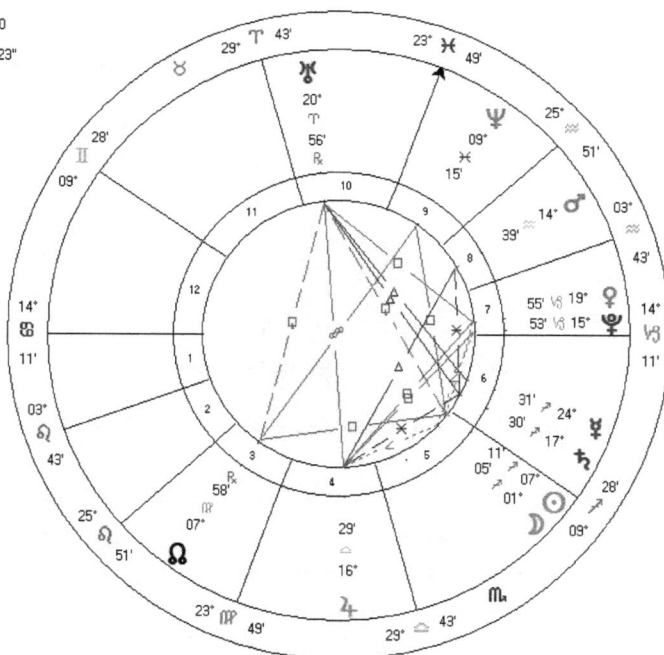

Figure 33 – New Moon November 29, 2016

Key dates to be alert to during this lunation include:

December 4 through 15 will feature sun at a 0 degree aspect to Saturn.

December 5: Moon will transit past NYSE co-ruler Mars.

December 6-7: Moon transits past NYSE co-ruler Neptune and also past the NYSE natal Mid-Heaven point of 24 Pisces.

Traders and investors should remain cognizant that on December 13-14, the FOMC Committee will meet and the meeting will be followed by Federal Reserve Governor Janet Yellen hosting a press conference.

December 15: Moon transits past the NYSE natal Ascendant point of 14 Cancer.

December 20: Mercury turns Retrograde.

December 21: Sun reaches its lowest declination point for the year.

January 2017

Key Dates

The New Moon cycle for January 2017 starts on December 28 with Sun at 7 degrees of Capricorn. The horoscope in Figure 34 depicts planetary placements several hours prior to the New Moon as the Ascendant passes 14 Cancer.

This lunation is intriguing in that both the NYSE co-ruling planets (Mars and Neptune) are conjunct together at 7 of Pisces. The lunation is a favorable 60 degrees aspect to this conjunct pairing. This is suggestive of a positive undertone for the NYSE.

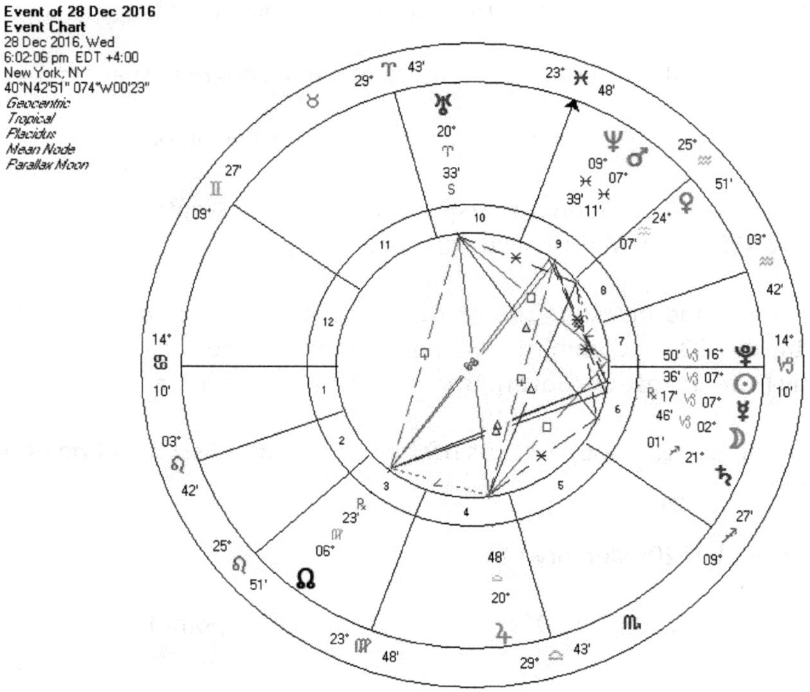

Event of 28 Dec 2016
Event Chart
28 Dec 2016, Wed
6:02:06 pm EDT +4:00
New York, NY
40°N42'51" 074°W00'23"
Geocentric
Tropical
Placidus
Mean Node
Parallax Moon

Figure 34 – New Moon December 28, 2016

Key dates to be alert to during this lunation include:

January 2-4: Moon will transit past NYSE co-rulers Mars and Neptune and also past the NYSE natal Mid-Heaven point of 24 Pisces.

January 11: Moon transits past the NYSE natal Ascendant point of 14 Cancer.

6. Astrology of Various Commodities in 2016

Gold

Investors who own Gold are accustomed to routinely checking the price of Gold by tuning into a television business channel or perhaps obtaining a live quote of Gold futures. But Gold is a unique entity - for working behind the scenes is an archaic methodology called the London Gold Fix.

The London Gold Fix occurs at 10:30 am and 3:00 pm local time each business day in London. Participants in the daily fixes are: Barclay's, HSBC, Scotia Mocatta (a division of Scotia Bank of Canada) and Societe Generale. These twice daily collaborations provide a benchmark price that is then used around the globe to settle and mark-to-market all the various Gold-related derivative contracts in existence.

The history of the Gold Fix is a fascinating one. On the 12th of September 1919, the Bank of England made arrangements with N.M. Rothschild & Sons for the formation of a free gold market in which there would be an official price for Gold quoted on any one day. At 11:00 am, the first Gold fixing took place, with the five principal gold bullion traders and refiners of the day performing the first gold fixing. These traders and refiners were N.M. Rothschild & Sons, Mocatta & Goldsmid, Pixley & Abell, Samuel Montagu & Co. and Sharps Wilkins.

The horoscope in Figure 35 depicts planetary positions at this date in history. Observations that jump off the page include:

North Node had just changed signs

Venus was Retrograde

Sun and Venus were conjunct

Mercury and Saturn were conjunct

Mars, Neptune and Jupiter were all conjunct
at/near the Mid-Heaven point of the horoscope

Saturn was 180 degrees opposite Uranus

London Gold Fix
Natal Chart
12 Sep 1919, Fri
11:00 am BST -1:00
London, United Kingdom
51°N30' 000°W10'
Geocentric
Tropical
Placidus
Mean Node
Parallax Moon

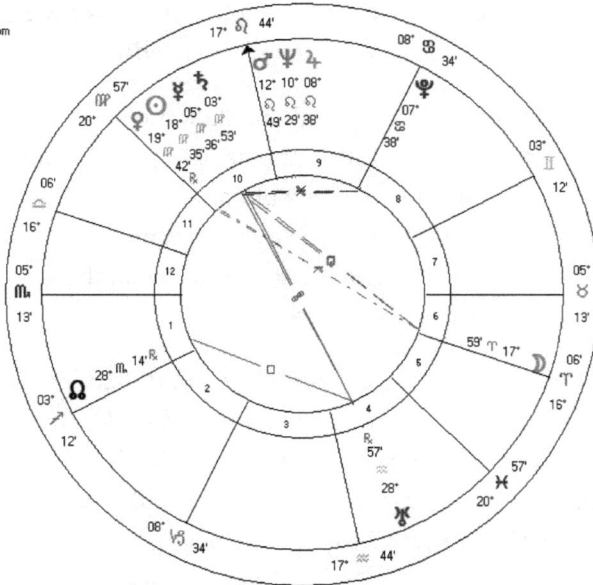

Figure 35   1919 London Gold Fix horoscope

Gold investors who have been around for a while will remember the
significant price peak recorded by Gold in January 1980. To illustrate how
astrology is linked to Gold prices consider that at this price peak, the
North Node had just changed signs and was 90 degrees hard aspect to the
natal Node in the 1919 horoscope. Consider too that Mars and Jupiter
were both coming into a 0 degree conjunction with the natal Sun location
in the 1919 horoscope. As the price of Gold was making its peak at nearly
$800/ounce, both Mars and Jupiter were turning Retrograde.

For those who were involved in Gold more recently, recall that Gold hit a significant peak in early September 2011 at just over $1900/ounce. At this peak, Sun and Venus were conjunct one another. What's more, they were within a few degrees of being conjunct to the natal Sun location in the 1919 horoscope.

In the few weeks that followed this peak, Gold prices plunged nearly $400/ounce. But, then Gold found its legs again and began to rally. This rally seems directly related to Mars being 90 degrees hard aspect to Jupiter. In addition, Mars was drawing into a 0 degree conjunction to the Mars-Jupiter-Neptune location of the 1919 horoscope wheel.

Such is the complex nature of Gold prices. I have studied past charts of Gold and I am shocked at how many price inflection points are related in one way or another to the astrology of the 1919 Gold Fix horoscope wheel. To those readers who are of the opinion that Gold price is manipulated – your notion is indeed a valid one and it is my firm belief that astrology is the secret language being spoken amongst those that play a hand in the manipulation.

But, traders and investors in Gold do not just rely on the daily London Fix for price indication. There is also the Gold futures market. Gold futures started trading on the New York Mercantile Exchange on December 31, 1974.

Figure 36 illustrates the planetary positions in 1974 at the first trade date of Gold futures. As an interesting exercise, note that in the 1919 chart Mars and Neptune are conjunct one another. Now, observe that Mars and Neptune are also conjunct in the 1974 chart. Next, ask yourself why the New York Mercantile Exchange would launch a new futures contract on December 31 – a time when most staff would be off for Christmas holidays. Take a look at the location of Moon in the 1974 horoscope. Moon is at 11 degrees of Leo. Now, take a look at the 1919 horoscope and observe that 11 degrees of Leo is where Mars and Neptune are located. I take these curious placements as further evidence of an astrological connection between Gold price, the 1919 Gold Fix date and the 1974 first trade date for Gold futures. All very intriguing stuff to be sure.

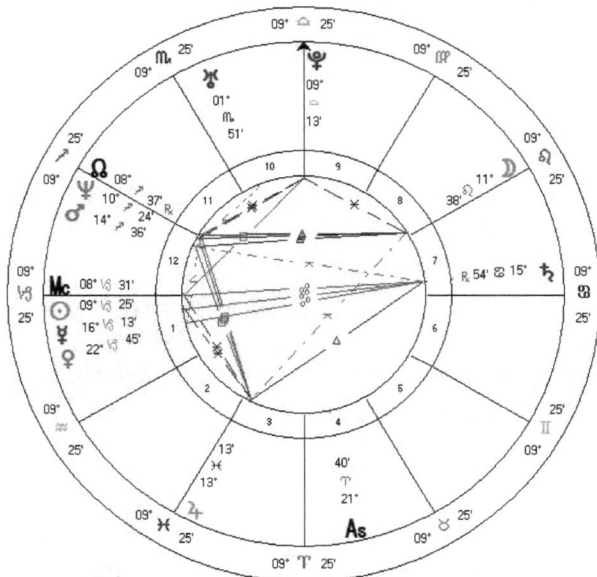

Gold Futures
Natal Chart
31 Dec 1974, Tue
11:59 am GMT +0:00
greenwich
51°N29' 000°W00'
Geocentric
Tropical
Sun on 1st
Mean Node
Parallax Moon

Figure 36 Gold futures first trade horoscope

Transiting Sun passing the natal Sun location from the 1974 first trade chart is a valuable tool for Gold trader to consider. Consider too, the 90 and 180 degree aspects. The chart in Figure 37 has been overlaid with 0, 90 and 180 degree aspects of transiting Sun / natal Sun. Note how these events align to various inflection points on the price chart.

For 2016, transiting Sun will make the following aspects to the 1974 natal Sun location:

January 1- January 6: passing 0 degrees conjunct to natal Sun

March 23-April 4: passing 90 degrees to natal Sun

June 24-July 6: passing 180 degrees to natal Sun

September 25-October 7: passing 90 degrees to natal Sun

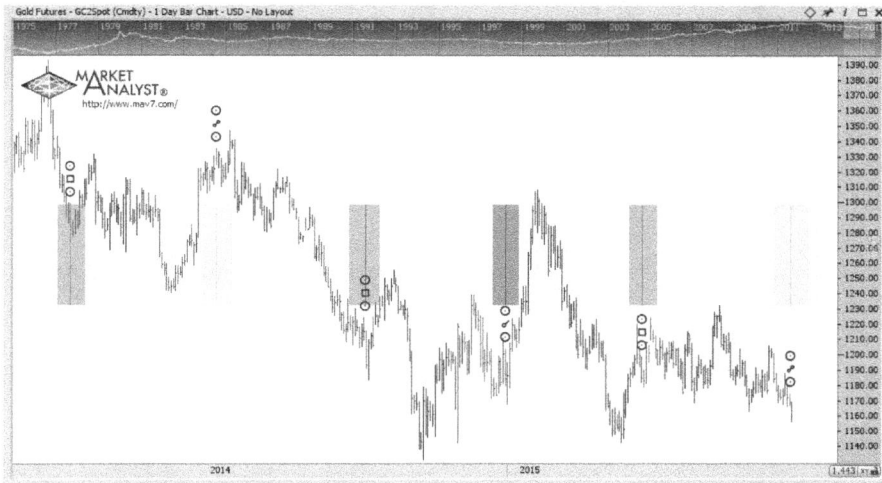

Figure 37 Transiting Sun / natal Sun aspects

Transiting Mars passing the natal Sun location from the 1974 first trade chart is a valuable tool for Gold trader to consider. Consider too, the 90 and 180 degree aspects. The chart in Figure 38 has been overlaid with 0, 90 and 180 degree aspects of transiting Mars / natal Sun. Note how these events align to various inflection points on the price chart.

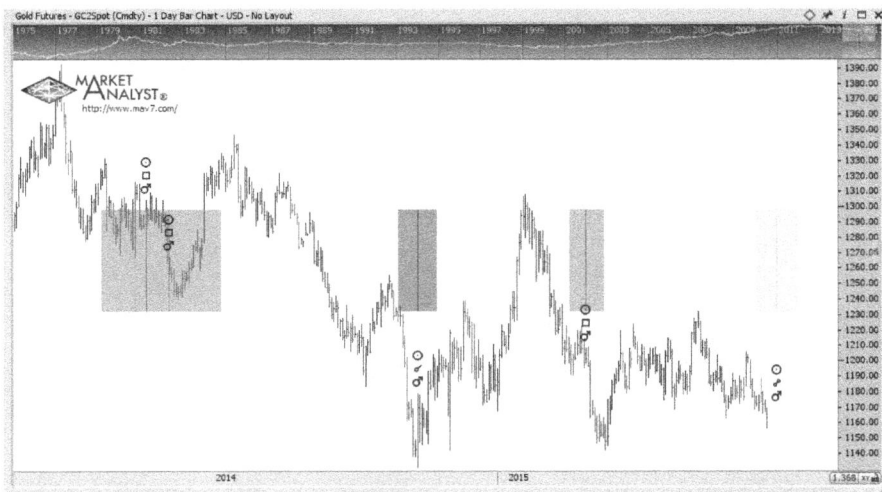

Figure 38 Transiting Mars / natal Sun aspects

For 2016, transiting Mars will make the following aspects to the 1974 natal Sun location:

September 30-October 19: passing 0 degrees conjunct to natal Sun

As previously noted, aspects to planetary locations in the 1919 Gold Fix horoscope are also important.

For 2016, transiting Sun will make the following aspects to the 1919 natal Sun location:

March 2-March 14: passing 180 degrees opposite to natal Sun

June 2-June 15: passing 90 degrees to natal Sun

September 2-September 19: passing 0 degrees conjunct to natal Sun

December 4-December 16: passing 90 degrees to natal Sun

Another cue from the 1919 chart is conjunctions between Sun and Venus. In 2016, Sun and Venus will be widely within orb of being conjunct from May 5 through July 3. The exact conjunction will occur June 8-10th.

Another valuable tool for Gold traders to consider is Mercury Retrograde events. In particular, watch for price action to suddenly break free from sideways consolidation patterns as Retrograde begins. Watch too for steep price inflection points during Retrograde.

The chart in Figure 39 illustrates the connection between these Mercury phenomena and Gold prices.

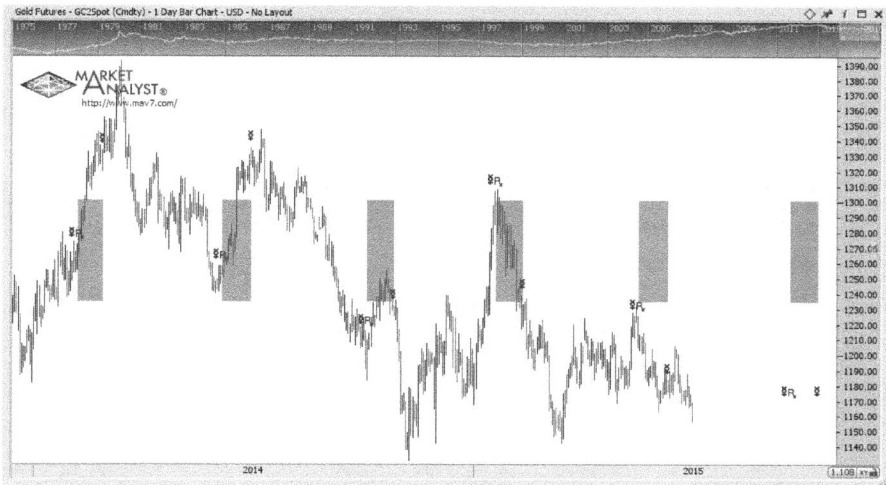

Figure 39 Gold and the Mercury Retrograde Influence

For 2016, Mercury will be Retrograde from January 6 through January 25, April 29 through May 22, August 31 through September 22 and December 20 through January 9, 2017.

Lastly, there is one additional cue to be taken from the 1919 horoscope chart. Notice that in this chart Saturn and Uranus are 180 degrees hard aspect opposite to one another. Times when Saturn and Uranus are 0, 90 or 180 degrees apart should be watched carefully. The last significant price peak on Gold came in September 2011 when these two heavyweight planets were opposite each other.

For 2016, there are no such hard aspects between these two planets.

The one question that I routinely get from those that follow my writings is – when during one of these astrological transit events should a person implement a trade? The answer is very simple. To reiterate what I have previously stated in this text - you should consider implementing a trade when you see the trend change. Always let the trend be your friend. You have heard this mantra before. I cannot emphasize it enough. There are many ways of measuring trend. My experience has shown me that the

83

methodologies developed by J. Welles Wilder are very powerful for identifying trend changes. In particular I prefer to use his Wilder Volatility Stop. Wilder's 1978 book *New Concepts in Technical Trading Systems* is a highly recommended read if you are seeking to learn more about his methods. Wilder wrote this book before the advent of computers. By working the examples in the book using a pencil and calculator, you will gain a deep appreciation for the mathematics associated with his indicators. This appreciation will then greatly aid you as you start to apply these indicators using your market trading software platform.

Silver

Silver futures started trading on a recognized financial exchange in 1933. Figure 40 shows the First Trade horoscope for Silver futures in geocentric format.

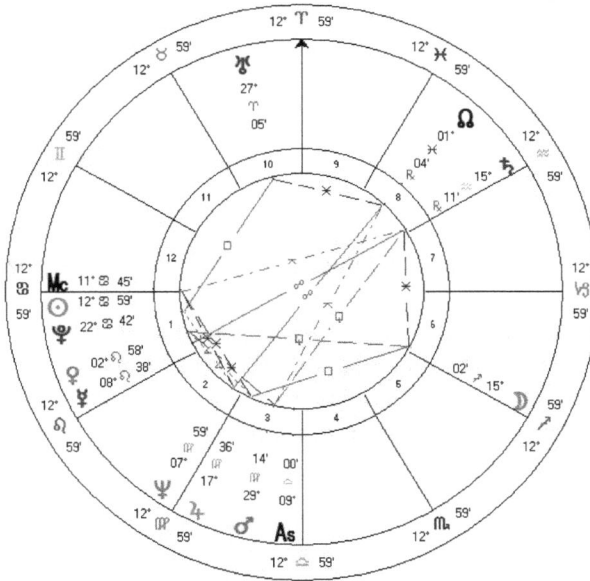

Figure 40 Silver futures First Trade horoscope

My research has shown that times when transiting Sun, transiting Mars and transiting Jupiter make hard aspects to the natal Sun point at 12 degrees Cancer should be watched carefully for evidence of trend changes and price inflection points. The daily Silver price chart in Figure 41 has been overlaid with times when transiting Sun makes 0, 90 and 180 degree aspects to the natal Sun position at 12 Cancer. Note how these events bear a good alignment to inflection points. Using a suitable measure of trend change (ie one of Wilder's methods), one would implement a trade during these Sun/natal Sun aspects if the trend recorded a change.

Figure 41 Silver and Sun/natal Sun events

The Silver price chart in Figure 42 has been overlaid with times when transiting Mars makes 0, 90 and 180 degree aspects to the natal Sun position. Using a suitable measure of trend change (ie one of Wilder's methods), one would implement a trade during these Sun/natal Sun aspects if the trend recorded a change.

Figure 42 Silver and Mars/natal Sun events

Planetary declinations should also be considered when studying price action of Silver futures. In particular the declination maxima and minima of Mars and also of Sun should be watched. Figures 43 and Figure 44 illustrate the effect of these declination events. As maxima and minima in declination draw near, use a suitable trend change indicator to assist you in your decision making.

Figure 43 Mars declination and Silver prices

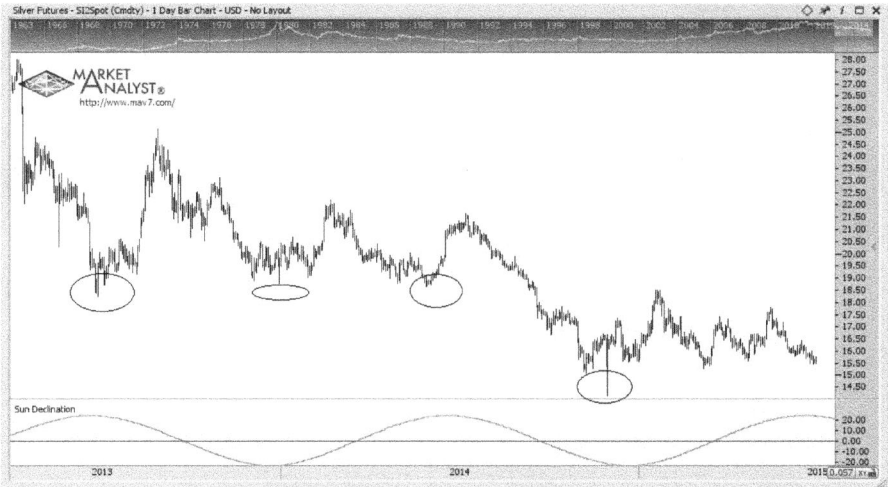

Figure 44 Sun declination and Silver prices

87

For 2016, Sun will make aspects to natal Sun as follows:

December 27, 2015 – January 8: Sun 180 degrees to natal Sun

March 25-April 7: Sun will pass 90 degrees to natal Sun

June 26-July 10: Sun will pass 0 degrees to natal Sun.

September 28-October 10: Sun passes 90 degrees to natal Sun.

For 2016, Mars will make aspects to natal Sun as follows:

October 4-October 22: Mars will pass 180 degrees to natal Sun.

For 2016, Sun will be at its maximum declination at the Summer Solstice on June 21. Sun will at its minimum declination at the Winter Solstice on Dec ember 21.

For 2016, Mars will exhibit its minimum declination in late September through early October.

Copper

The First Trade Date for Copper futures was July 29, 1988. Figure 45 illustrates the First Trade horoscope in geocentric format.

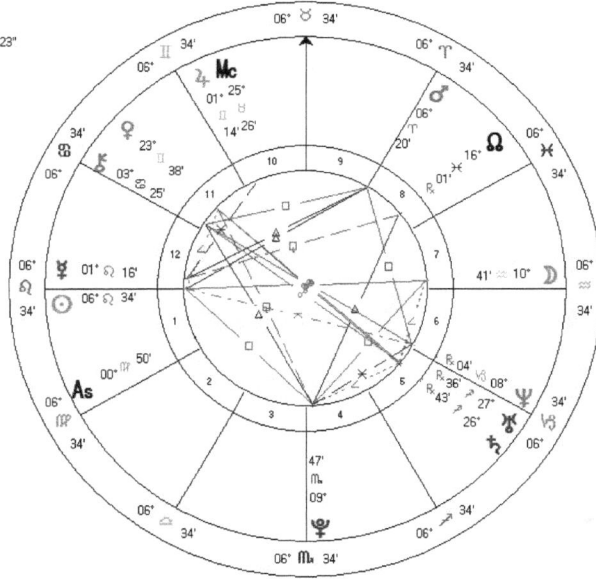

Figure 45 Copper futures First Trade horoscope

This horoscope wheel features an Inferior Conjunction of Mercury in the sign of Leo.

Also, notice in this horoscope that the First Trade date is that of a Full Moon.

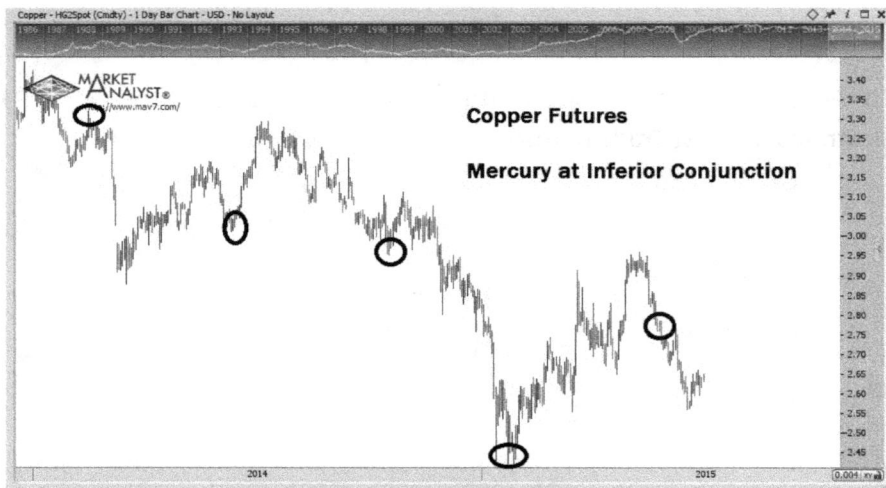

Figure 46 Copper and Mercury Inferior Conjunction events

The daily price chart for Copper futures in Figure 46 has been overlaid with Mercury Inferior Conjunction events. Knowing that such an event is approaching, one should watch a suitable price chart technical indicator for evidence of a short term trend change.

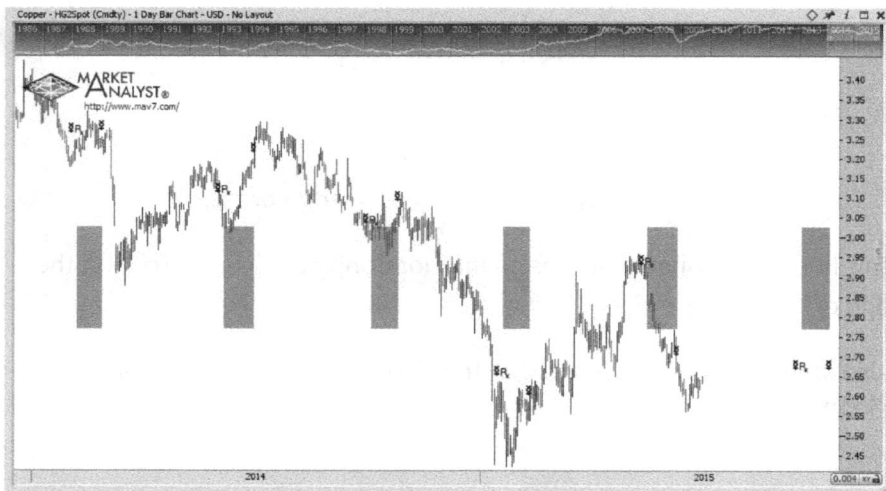

Figure 47 Copper and Mercury Retrograde events

Mercury Inferior Conjunction events always occur in association with Mercury being Retrograde. The Copper price chart in Figure 47 has been overlaid with Retrograde events.

For 2016, Mercury will be Retrograde from:

January 6 through January 25, April 29 through May 22, August 31 through September 22 and December 20 through January 9, 2017

During 2016, Mercury will be at Inferior Conjunction on January 14, May 9, September 13 and December 28.

Traders following Copper should remain alert to dates of New and Full Moons. In studying Copper price charts going back several years I have noticed that the Wilder Volatility Stop has a high propensity to deliver a trend change indication at New and Full Moons.

Canadian Dollar, British Pound and Japanese Yen

These three futures instruments all started trading on May 16th, 1972 at the Chicago Mercantile Exchange. The horoscope in Figure 48 illustrates planetary placements at this date. There are no significant aspects to the Sun evident in this horoscope. It is interesting to note, however, that Mars is 180 degrees opposite Jupiter. This suggests that Mars and Jupiter may play a role in price fluctuations on these currencies. Mars is also 0 degrees conjunct to Venus, suggesting another cyclical relationship.

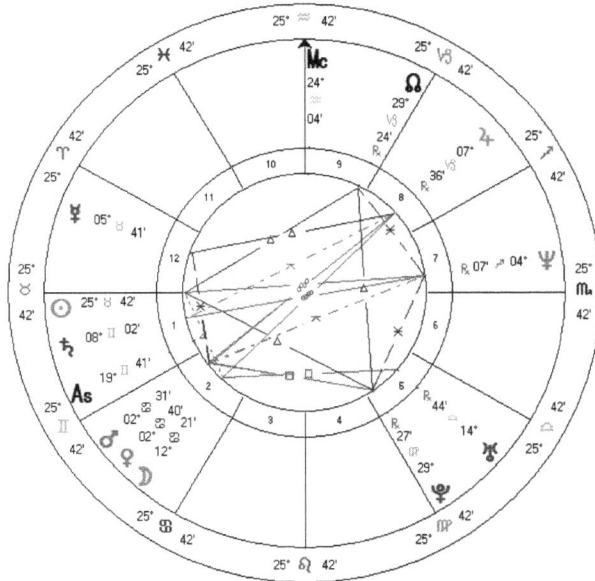

Figure 48 Pound, Yen, Canadian First Trade horoscope

The chart in Figure 49 illustrates price action on the Canadian Dollar. Mars conjunct Venus events only occur every couple years. As this chart shows, such an event occurred in early 2015 and as it did, the Canadian Dollar registered a low and a change of trend.

Figure 49 Canadian Dollar Mars conjunct Venus

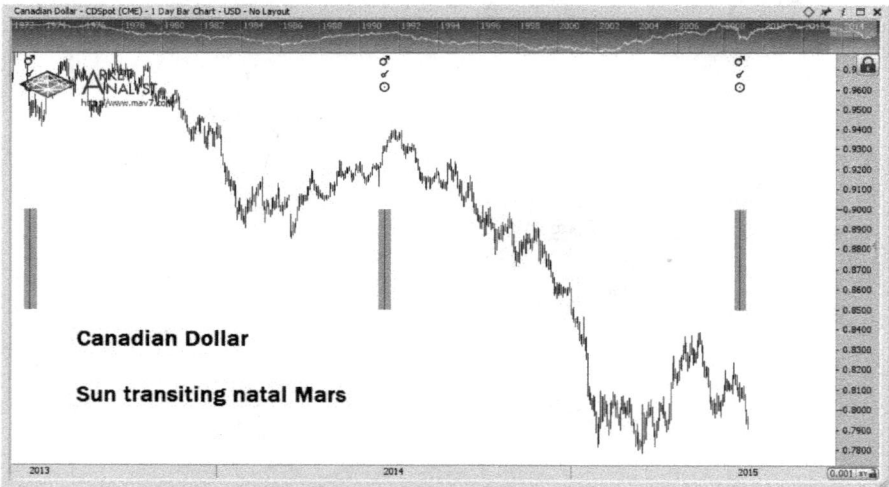

Figure 50 Canadian Dollar Sun passing natal Mars

The chart in Figure 50 illustrates the effect of transiting Sun passing natal Mars (2 degrees of Cancer in the 1972 horoscope chart).

The chart in Figure 51 illustrates the effect of transiting Sun passing natal Jupiter.

Figure 51 British Pound Sun passing natal Jupiter

Mercury retrograde events also bear a good alignment to trend changes on the Pound, Yen and Canadian.

The Yen price chart in Figure 51 has been overlaid with Mercury Retrograde events. Traders are advised to use a suitable trend change chart indicator to watch for actionable trend changes during Retrograde events.

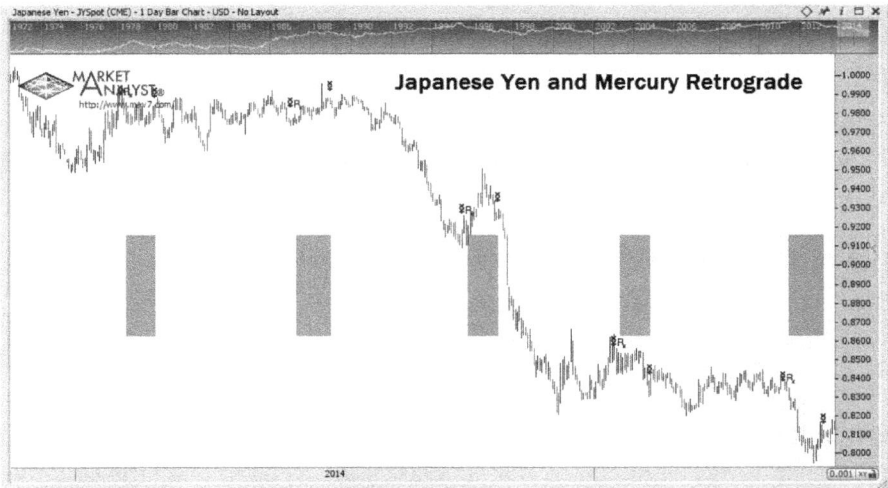

Figure 52 Yen and Mercury Retrograde

For 2016, there are no Mars conjunct Venus events.

For 2016, transiting Sun will make hard aspects to the natal Mars point of 2 degrees Cancer as follows:

March 16 to March 28: 90 degrees square

June 16 to June 29: 0 degrees conjunct

September 17 to September 30: 90 degrees square

December 16 to December 30: 180 degrees opposite

For 2016, transiting Sun will make hard aspects to the natal Jupiter point of 7 degrees Capricorn as follows:

March 20 to April 2: 90 degrees square

June 21 to July 5: 10 degrees opposite

September 22 to October 7: 90 degrees square

December 21 to January 4, 2017: 0 degrees conjunct

For 2016, Mercury will be Retrograde from:

January 6 through January 25, April 29 through May 22, August 31 through September 22 and December 20 through January 9, 2017

During 2016, Mercury will be at Inferior Conjunction on January 14, May 9, September 13 and December 28.

Planetary declination can also be used as a tool by currency traders. In particular, times when Venus is at its maximum declination all too often align to trend inflection points on the Pound, Yen and Canadian.

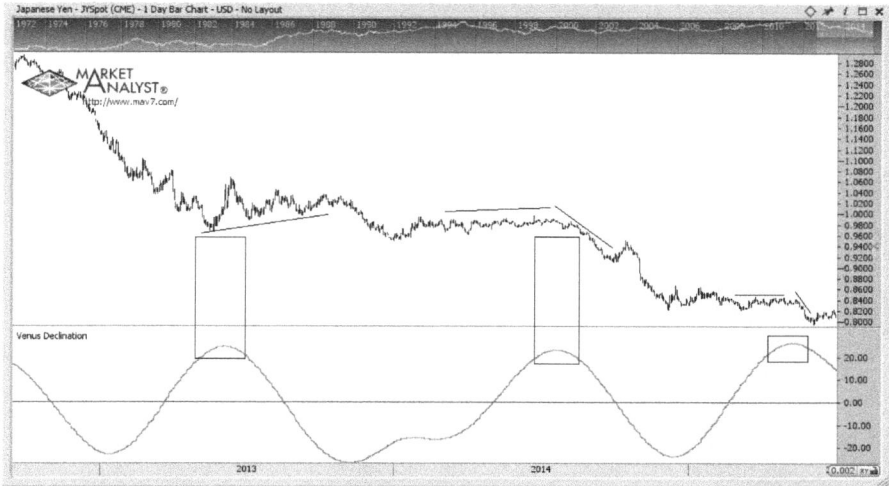

Figure 53 Yen and Venus Declination

The Yen chart in Figure 53 has been amended to include a Venus declination plot in the lower panel. Observe how Venus declination maxima co-incide with trend changes of varying magnitude. A similar relation holds for the Pound and the Canadian Dollar.

For 2016, Venus will record its maximum declination during the 10 days either side of its exact maximum on June 20.

Euro Currency Futures

The Euro became the official currency for the European Union on January 1, 2002 when Euro bank notes became freely and widely circulated. Arguably there may be another date – January 1999 when the E.U. zone nations were required to establish a fixed rate of exchange between their currencies and the Euro currency. But, I prefer the 2002 date because of the peculiar relation between Venus and Sun. A look at the geocentric natal First Trade horoscope for this date in Figure 54 reveals Sun and Venus are very near to Superior Conjunction. In fact, the exact date of Superior Conjunction was January 14, 2002.

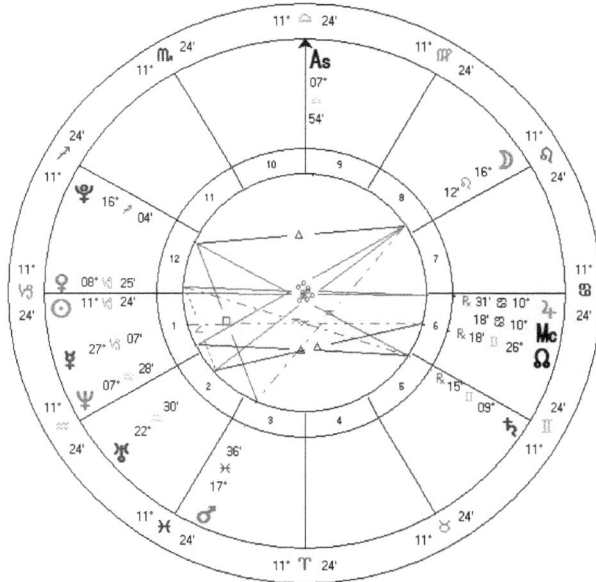

Figure 54 Euro Currency First Trade horoscope

Venus Superior Conjunction events can be used as a tool to assist traders and investors with decision making. The chart of the Euro currency in Figure 55 has been overlaid with Superior Conjunction events. As Figure 55 shows, a brief period of Euro weakness in 2013 ended at a Venus

Superior Conjunction. In 2014 a more significant decline in the Euro tried to rectify itself, but failed to do so. Then, the downtrend took on a more dire note after the Venus Superior Conjunction event.

Figure 55 Venus Superior Conjunction and the Euro

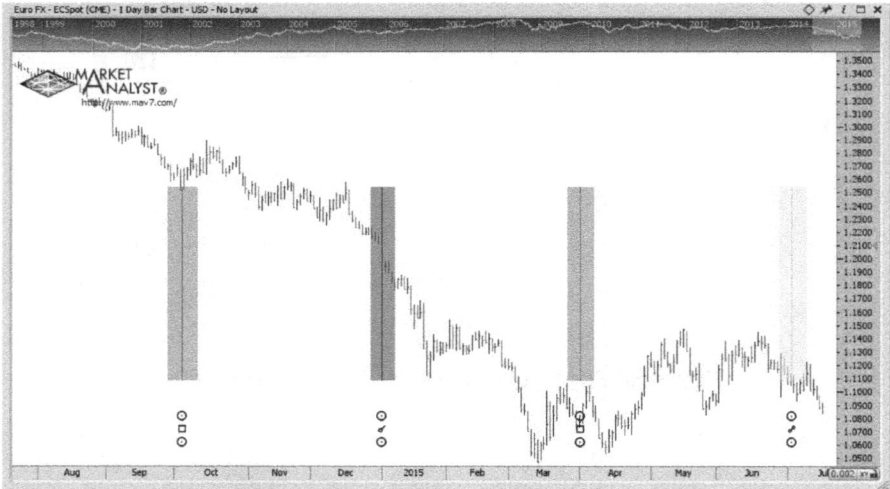

Figure 56 Astro events and the Euro Currency

The traditional McWhirter approach can also be applied to the Euro currency. The chart in Figure 56 has been overlaid with events of transiting Sun making 0, 90 and 180 degree aspects to the natal Sun position in the Euro 2002 First Trade chart. Traders of the Euro currency should remain aware that Sun/natal Sun aspects can and often do align to inflection points.

For 2016, Venus will be at Superior Conjunction again on June 6, 2016.

For 2016, transiting Sun will be 0 degrees conjunct natal Sun during the first week of January. Transiting Sun will be 90 degrees natal Sun March 26 through April 7. Transiting Sun will be 180 degrees opposite natal Sun from June 22 through July 12. Transiting Sun will again be 90 degrees to natal Sun from 28 of September through October 9.

Australian Dollar

Australian dollar futures started trading on the Chicago Mercantile Exchange on January 13, 1987. As the horoscope in Figure 57 shows, Sun and Mercury are at a Superior Conjunction at 22-23 degrees Capricorn.

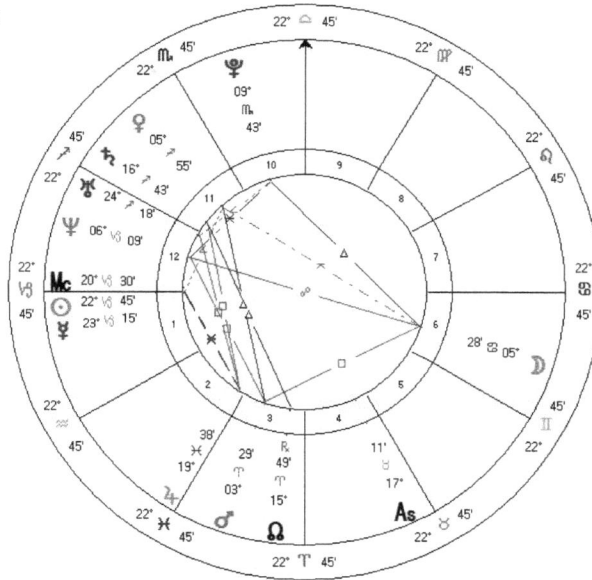

Figure 57 First Trade horoscope for Australian Dollar Futures

The chart in Figure 58 has been overlaid with Mercury Superior and Inferior conjunction events. Traders of Aussie Dollar futures should remain aware that these Mercury conjunction events often do align to inflection points.

Mercury Retrograde events also have a strong tendency to align to price inflection points on the Aussie Dollar as the chart in Figure 59 illustrates.

 These inflection points will vary in magnitude and could occur immediately before, during or immediately after a Mercury Retrograde event. Diligence on your part is required.

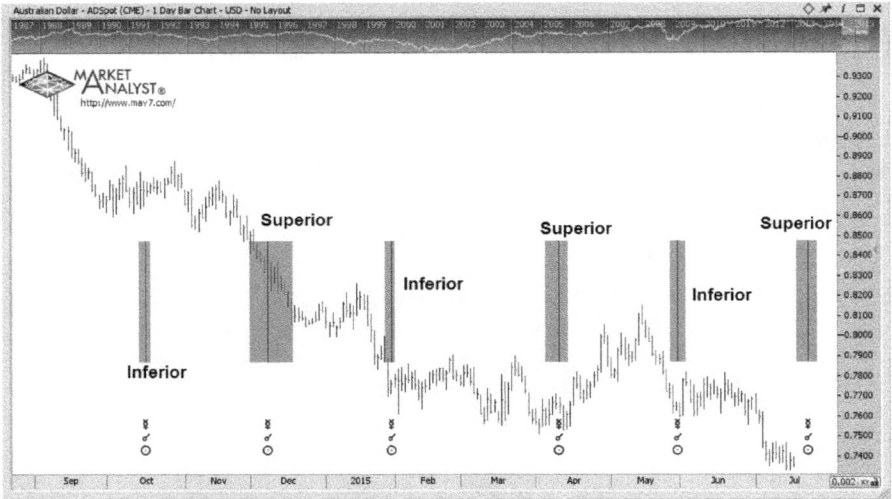

Figure 58 Australian Dollar and Mercury Conjunctions

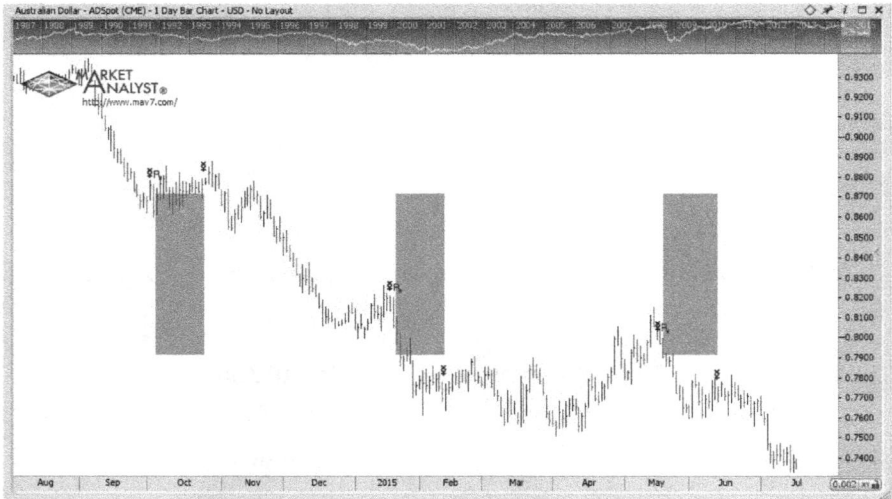

Figure 59 Australian Dollar and Mercury Retrograde

The use of a chart technical indicator to measure short term trend change is also highly advised.

For 2016, Mercury will be Retrograde from:

January 6 through January 25

April 29 through May 22

August 31 through September 22

December 20 through January 9, 2017

The traditional McWhirter approach can also be applied to the Aussie Dollar. The price chart in Figure 60 has been overlaid with events of transiting Sun making 0, 90 and 180 degree hard aspects to the natal Sun position of 22 Capricorn from the 1987 First Trade chart.

Figure 60 Australian Dollar and Sun/natal Sun events

For 2016, transiting Sun will make 0, 90, and 180 degree aspects to natal Sun on:

January 5 through January 21
April 6 through April 18
July 6 through July 25
October 9 through October 21

30 Year Bond Futures

30 Year Bond futures started trading in Chicago on August 22, 1977. Figure 61 presents the geocentric First Trade horoscope for this date.

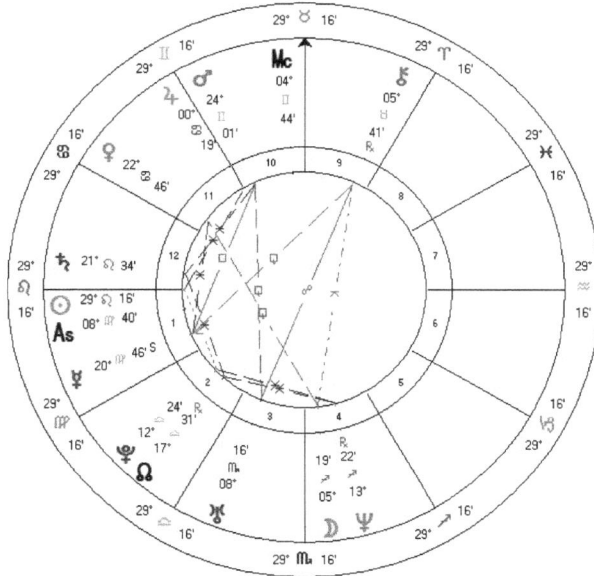

30 Year Bonds
Natal Chart
22 Aug 1977, Mon
11:59 am GMT +0:00
Chicago, Illinois
41°N51' 087°W39'
Geocentric
Tropical
Sun on 1st
Mean Node
Parallax Moon

Figure 61 First Trade horoscope for 30 Year Bond futures

The traditional McWhirter approach can be used to provide a roadmap of sorts for the 30 Year Bonds. The price chart in Figure 62 has been overlaid with events of transiting Sun passing the natal Jupiter position of 0 degrees Cancer. There is a strong propensity for these aspects to align to price inflection points. Traders of the 30 Year Bonds futures are advised to incorporate this information with a suitable technical trend indicator.

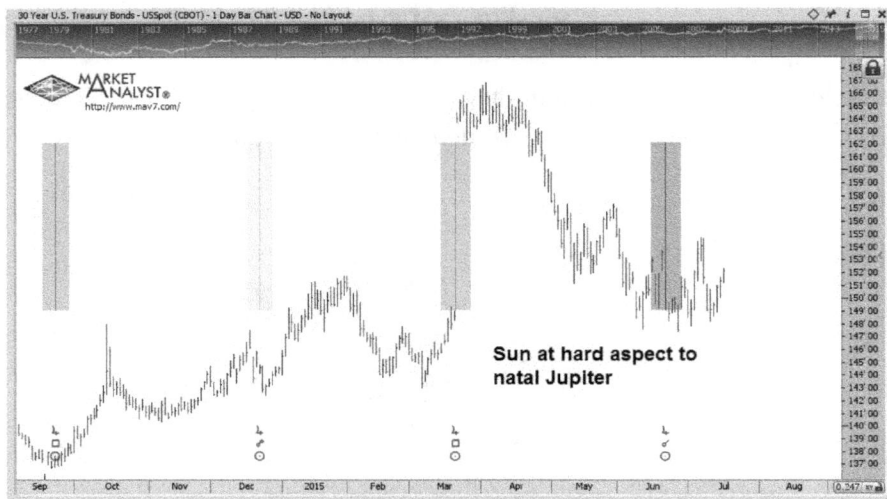

Figure 62 Bonds (30 Year) and Sun in aspect to natal Jupiter

Look closely at the First Trade horoscope in Figure 61 and you will note that the position of Mercury is further delineated by a letter' S'. This means *stationary direct. A* planet that is stationary direct is about to turn Retrograde. I find it curious that the regulatory authorities would conceive of a First Trade date that was one day prior to Mercury turning Retrograde. Herein lies a strong hint. The price chart in Figure 63 has been overlaid with Mercury Retrograde events. Note the propensity for short term inflections in trend at these Retrograde events.

For 2016, transiting Sun will make hard 0, 90 or 180 degree aspects to natal Jupiter on:

January 1 through January 4, transiting Sun will be completing a 180 degree hard aspect.

March 16 through March 25, transiting Sun will make a 90 degree aspect

June 12 through July 1, transiting Sun will make a 0 degree aspect.

September 17 through September 30, transiting Sun will make a 90 degree aspect.

Figure 63 Bonds (30 Year) and Mercury Retrograde

For 2016, Mercury will be Retrograde from:

January 6 through January 25

April 29 through May 22

August 31 through September 22

December 20 through January 9, 2017

My research has also shown that New Moons and Full Moons also affect Bond prices.

The chart in Figure 64 presents 30 Year Bond price data with New Moon and Full Moon dates indicated.

Figure 64 Bond Futures and Moon Phase

For 2016, New Moon dates are January 10, February 8, March 9, April 7, May 6, June 5, July 4, August 2, September 1, October 1, October 30, November 29 and December 29.

For 2016, Full Moon dates are January 24, February 22, March 23, April 22, May 21, June 20, July 19, August 18, September 16, October 16, November 14 and December 14.

The Bond story has one additional layer to it. Authors Jeanne Long and Larry Pesavento, whose material I have researched for my previous books, are adamant that changes in Bond prices can be seen to align to geocentric Mars changing signs of the zodiac.

Mars will change signs approximately every seven weeks. The reason for this correlation to sign changes remains unclear to me. My research has shown that this phenomenon does align to trend changes, but not with 100% correlation.

For 2016, geocentric Mars will change signs of the zodiac on:

January 4 when it moves into Scorpio.

March 7 when it moves into Sagittarius.

August 3 when it moves into Sagittarius after having been Retrograde.

September 8 when it moves into Capricorn.

November 10 when it moves in Aquarius.

December 20 when it moves into Pisces.

10 Year Treasury Note Futures

10 Year Treasury Notes started trading in Chicago on May 3, 1982. Figure 65 presents the geocentric First Trade horoscope for this date.

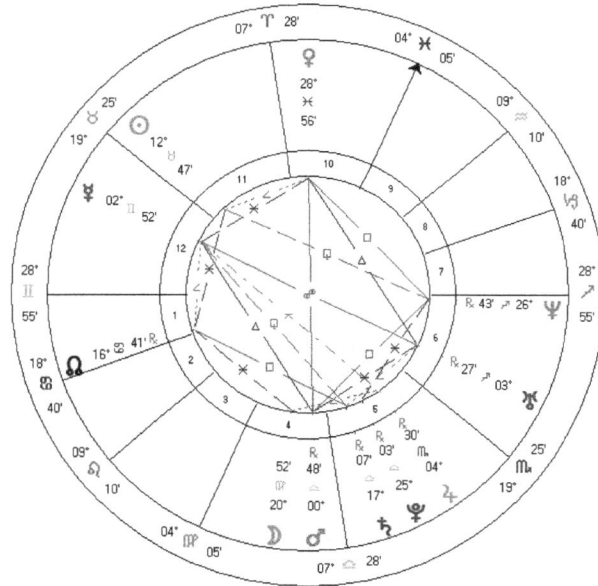

10 Year Treasury Note
Natal Chart
3 May 1982, Mon
8:30 am CDT +5:00
chicago, Illinois
41°N51' 087°W39'
Geocentric
Tropical
Placidus
Mean Node
Parallax Moon

Figure 65 First Trade horoscope for 10 Year Treasury Notes

Note the peculiar rectangle pattern formed by the corner points of Mercury, Venus, Mars and Uranus.

My research has shown that times when aggressive planet Mars passes by the natal Sun position or even the natal Venus and natal Mercury locations can align trend changes on a short term basis. Traders using this correlation are advised to also be using a suitable technical chart trend indicator tool. Figure 66 shows a 10 Year Treasury chart overlaid with Mars/natal Sun events. Figure 67 depicts Mars making 0 degree aspects to natal Venus and natal Mercury positions.

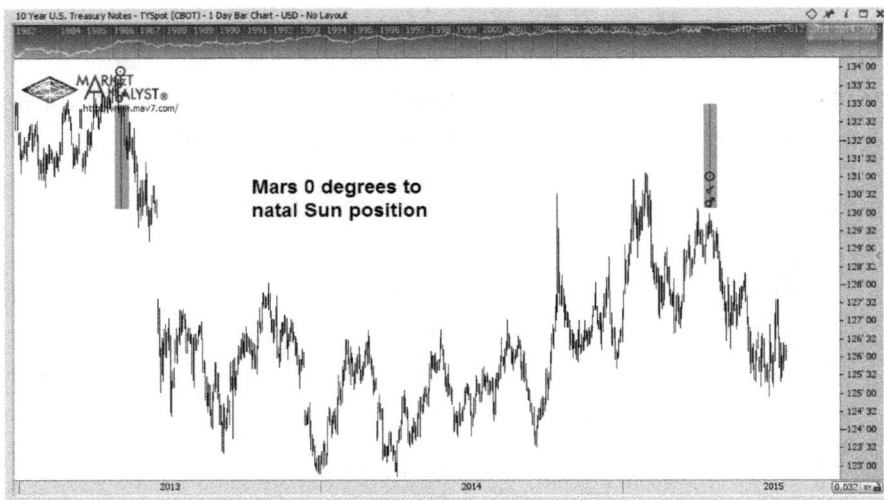

Figure 66 Mars/natal Sun events and 10 Year Treasury Notes

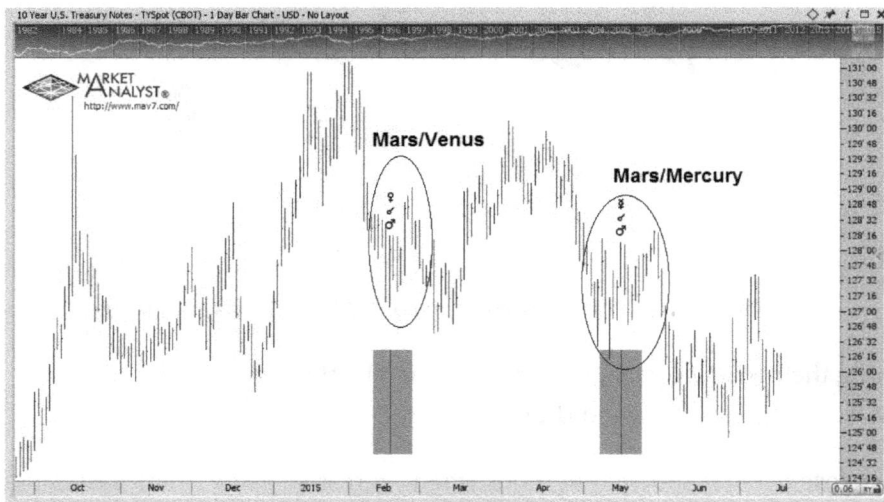

Figure 67 Mars/natal Venus and Mercury events

My research has also shown that Mercury Retrograde events all too often align to short term trend change pivots. The price chart in Figure 68 depicts the effect of Mercury retrograde events on the 10 Year Notes.

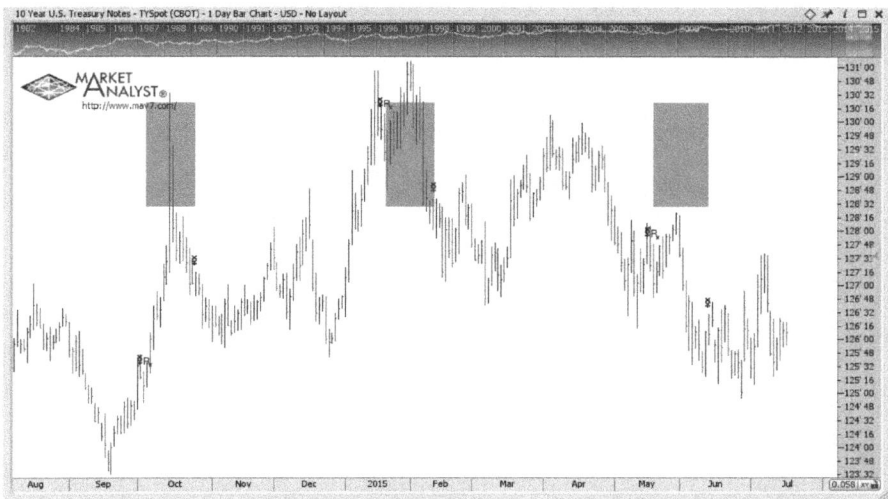

Figure 68 Mercury Retrograde and 10 Year Treasury Notes

For 2016, Mercury will be Retrograde from:

January 6 through January 25

April 29 through May 22

August 31 through September 22

December 20 through January 9, 2017

Mars will transit 0 degrees conjunct to the natal Uranus point of 3 Sagittarius from July 26 to August 15, 2016. There will be no transits of Mars past the natal Sun, Venus or Mercury positions in 2016. For 2016, the Mercury Retrograde events will represent the best opportunities for short term traders.

Wheat, Corn, Oats

Wheat, Corn and Oats futures all share the same First Trade date from 1877. The horoscope in Figure 69 shows planetary placements at this date.

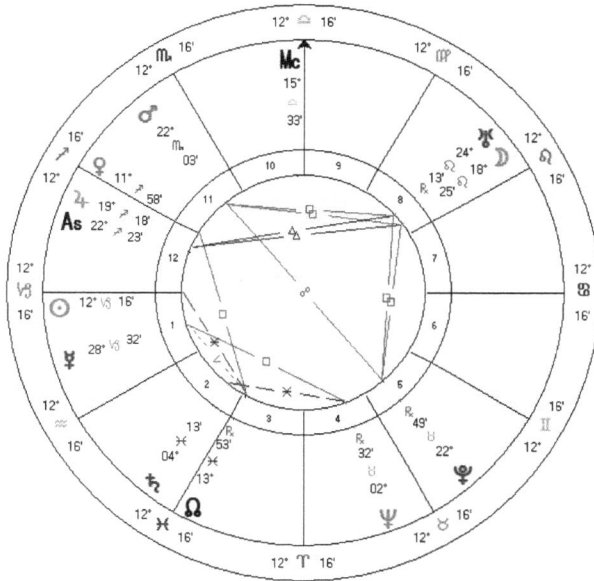

Figure 69 First Trade horoscope for Wheat, Corn and Oats futures

Basic McWhirter astrology is a useful tool to help traders navigate often volatile price action of Wheat, Corn and Oats. To illustrate, the Corn price chart in Figure 70 has been overlaid with events of transiting Sun making 0, 90 and 180 degree aspects to the natal Sun position in the 1877 First Trade horoscope. Figure 71 illustrates the effect of transiting Mars making hard aspects to the natal Sun position. The application of a chart technical indicator to monitor short term trend changes is essential if relying on any such McWhirter astrology events.

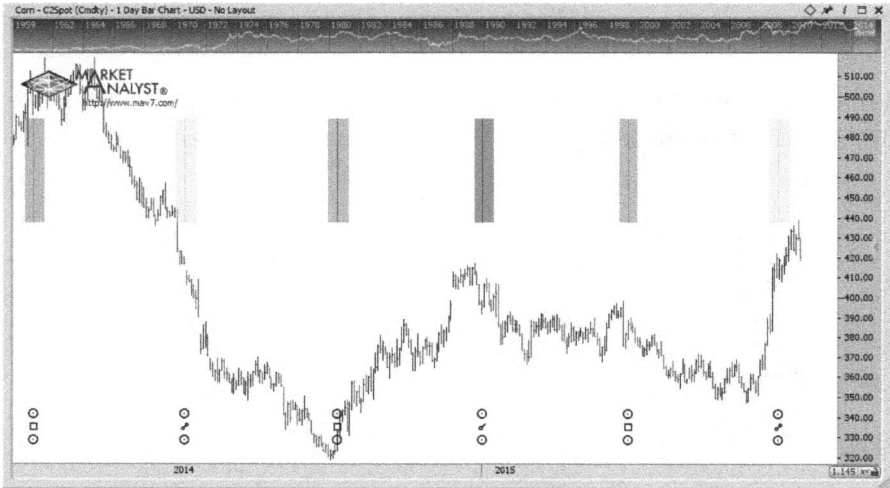

Figure 70 Corn prices and Sun/natal Sun events

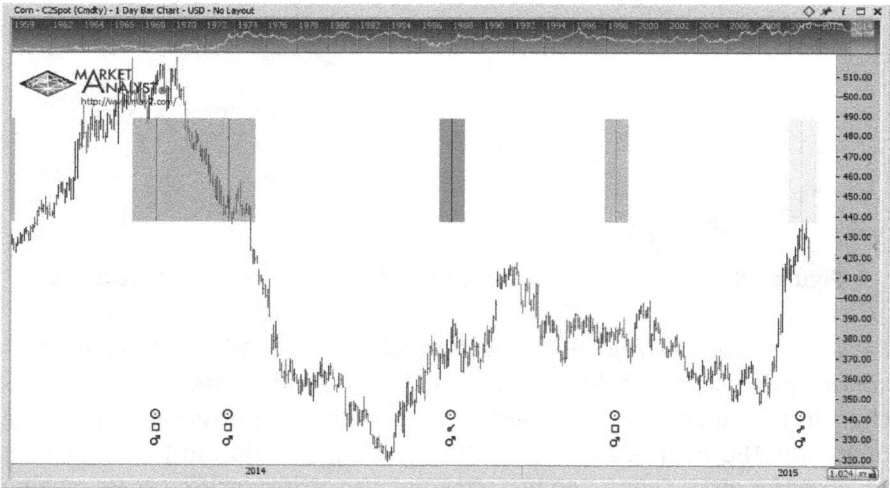

Figure 71 Corn prices and Mars/natal Sun events

Planetary declination also is a powerful tool that can be used to help traders identify the coming of trend reversals. Figures 72 and 73 illustrate the application of declination to price charts.

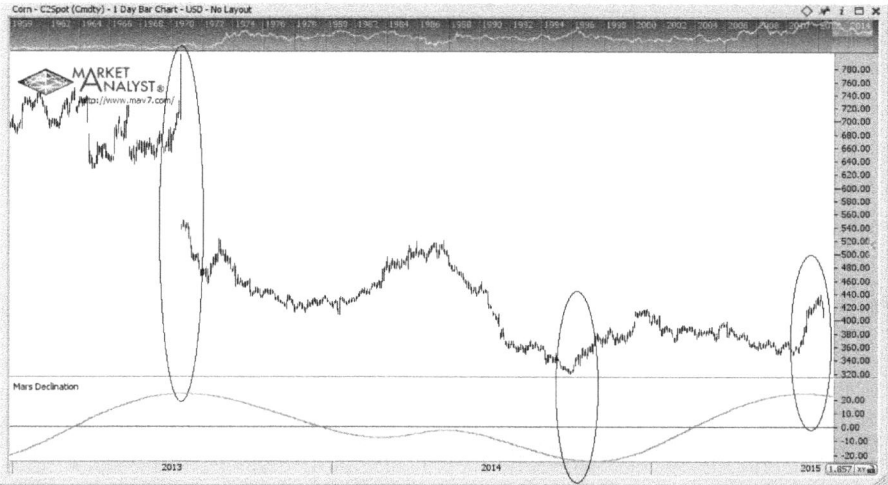

Figure 72 Corn prices and Mars declination

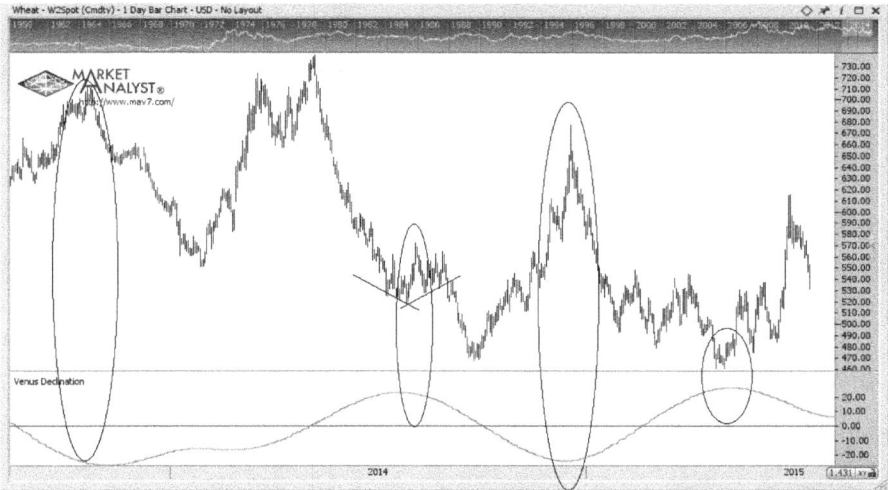

Figure 73 Wheat prices and Venus declination

If using declination as a tool, be sure to always use the geocentric declination. Also be sure to also apply a suitable chart technical indicator to help identify trend changes. Also, note that trend changes could be very short lived or also more substantial.

My research has also shown that Mercury plays a role in price pivot points on the grains. The price chart of Corn futures in Figure 74 has been overlaid with Mercury Retrograde events. Not all Retrograde events will automatically align to a trend change. The propensity for such trend changes are however significant. The use of a suitable chart technical indicator is strongly recommended. Although not shown here, Mercury Retrograde events do have a similar propensity to align to trend changes on Wheat prices.

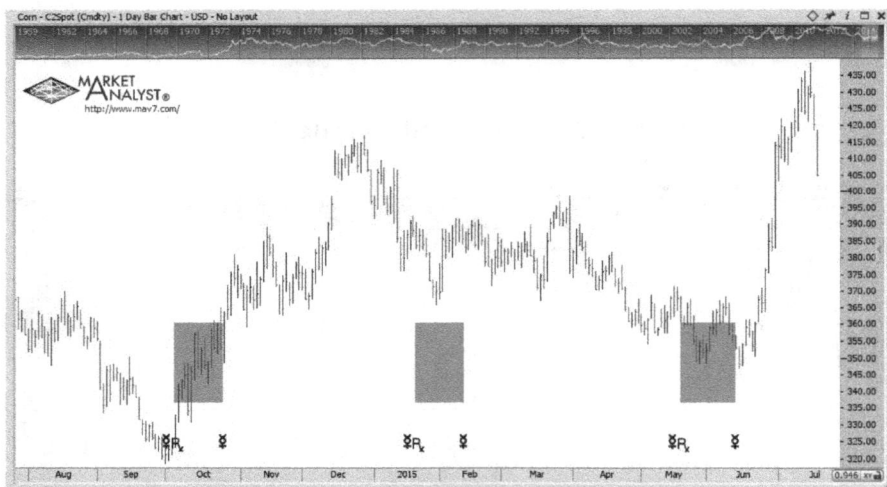

Figure 74 Corn prices and Mercury Retrograde events

For 2016, transiting Sun will be 0 degree to natal Sun from January 1 through January 8.

Sun will be 90 degrees natal Sun from March 27 through April 8.

Sun will be 180 degrees natal Sun from June 26 through July 11.

Sun will be 90 degrees natal Sun from September 29 through October 11.

Mars will be 0 degrees natal Sun from October 7 through October 23.

For 2016, Mercury will be Retrograde from:

January 6 through January 25

April 29 through May 22

August 31 through September 22

December 20 through January 9, 2017

For 2016, Venus will be at its minimum declination from January 17 through February 6. Venus will cross 0 degrees declination at April 8. Its maximum declination will occur June 12 through June 30. August 31 will see 0 degrees declination again. November 8 through 24 will see minimum declination.

For 2016, the month of September will see Mars carve out its minimum declination for the year.

Soybeans

Soybean futures started trading in Chicago on October 5, 1936. The horoscope in Figure 75 illustrates the planetary placements at that time. What I find intriguing is the location of the Sun. Notice how it is exactly 90 degrees to the location of the Sun in the First Trade chart for Wheat, Corn and Oats? As I have previously noted, the regulatory officials who determine these First Trade dates seem to know more about Astrology than you may think.

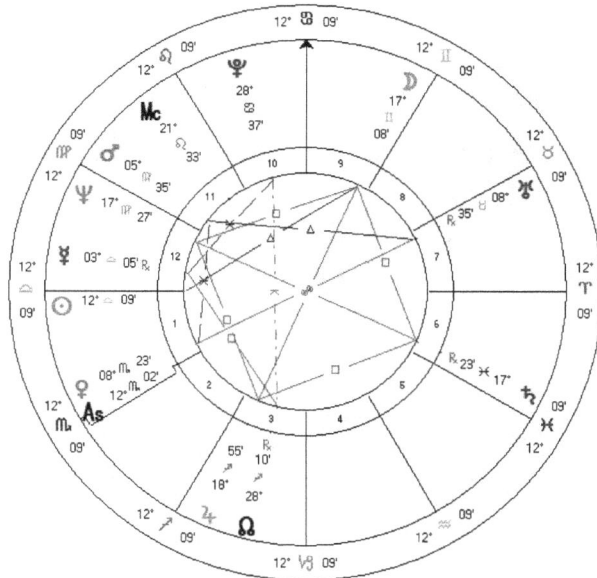

Figure 75 Soybeans First Trade horoscope

Basic McWhirter astrology is a useful tool to help traders navigate often volatile price action of Soybeans. To illustrate, the Soybeans price chart in Figure 76 has been overlaid with events of transiting Sun making 0, 90 and 180 degree aspects to the natal Sun position in the 1936 First Trade horoscope. Figure 77 illustrates the effect of transiting Mars making hard aspects to the natal Sun position. The application of a chart technical indicator to monitor short term trend changes is essential if relying on any such McWhirter astrology events.

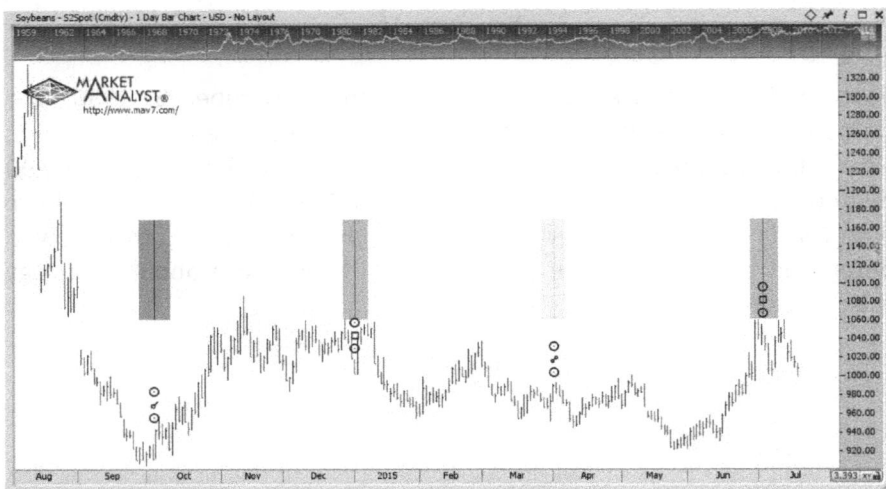

Figure 76 Soybeans and Sun/natal Sun events

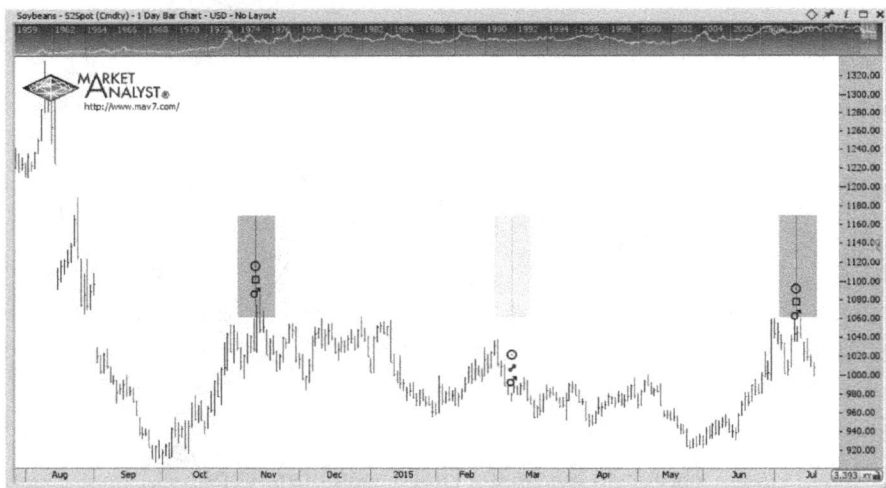

Figure 77 Soybeans and Mars/natal Sun events

For 2016, transiting Sun will make a 90 degree aspect to natal Sun from January 1 through January 8.

Transiting Sun will make a 180 degree aspect to natal Sun from March 25 through April 8.

A 90 degree aspect to natal Sun will occur from June 28 through July 11.

A 0 degree aspect will occur from September 26 through October 12.

Transiting Mars will make a 90 degree aspect to natal Sun from October 6 through October 24.

Soybean traders should also be alert to the fact that in 2016, positive, expansive planet Jupiter will transit 0 degrees to the natal Sun position during October and November.

Mercury Retrograde events also contribute to the price behavior of Soybeans. The Soybeans chart in Figure 78 illustrates the Mercury Retrograde effect. If there is a trend change associated with Mercury Retrograde, the trend change may come immediately beforehand, during or immediately after the retrograde event. Diligence on your part will be required. The use of a suitable chart technical indicator will be essential to help identify the trend shifts.

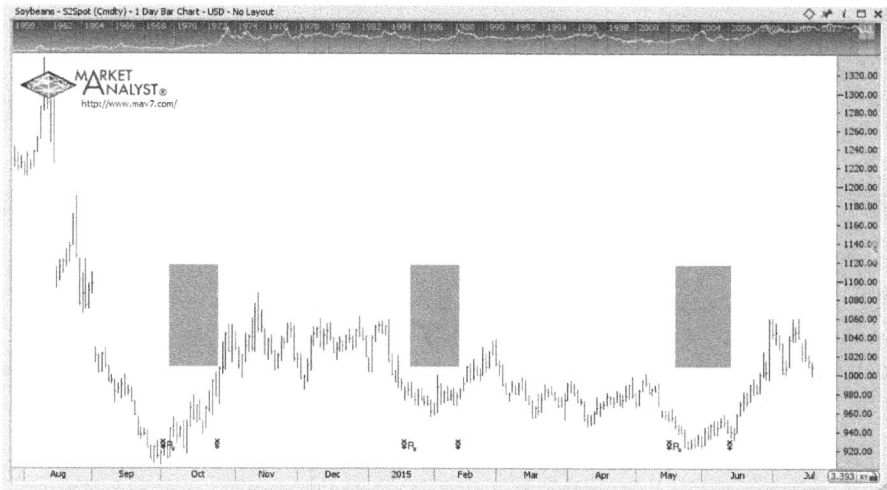

Figure 78 Soybeans and Mercury events

For 2016, Mercury will be Retrograde from:

January 6 through January 25

April 29 through May 22

August 31 through September 22

December 20 through January 9, 2017

Soybeans also have a tendency to record price trend changes in proximity to Mars and Venus recording maximum, zero and minimum declinations. The Soybean price charts in Figures 79 and 80 illustrate further.

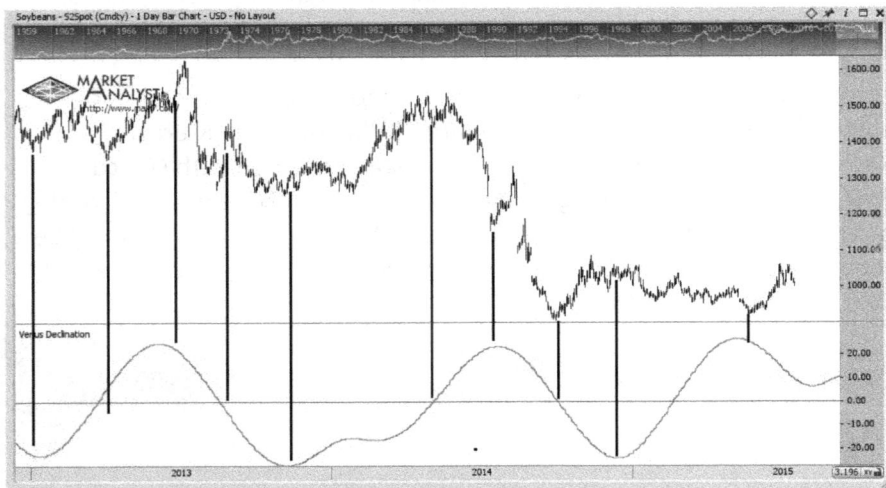

Figure 79 Soybeans and Venus Declination

For 2016, Venus will be at its minimum declination from January 17 through February 6. Venus will cross 0 degrees declination at April 8. Its maximum declination will occur June 12 through June 30. August 31 will see 0 degrees declination again. November 8 through 24 will see minimum declination.

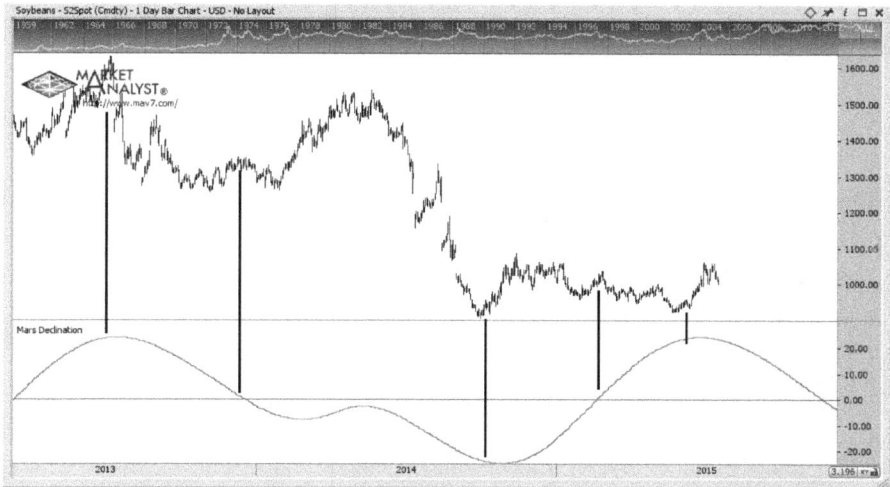

Figure 80 Soybeans and Mars Declination

If using declination to identify trend changes, it must be noted that the trend change may not always occur precisely at the maximum, zero or minimum declination level. The use of a chart technical indicator to help identify a trend change is essential.

For 2016, the month of September will see Mars carve out its minimum declination for the year.

Crude Oil

West Texas Intermediate Crude Oil futures started trading on a recognized exchange for the first time on March 30, 1983. A unique alignment of celestial points can be seen in the horoscope in Figure 81. Notice how Mars, North Node, (Saturn/Pluto/Moon) and Neptune conspire to form a rectangle.

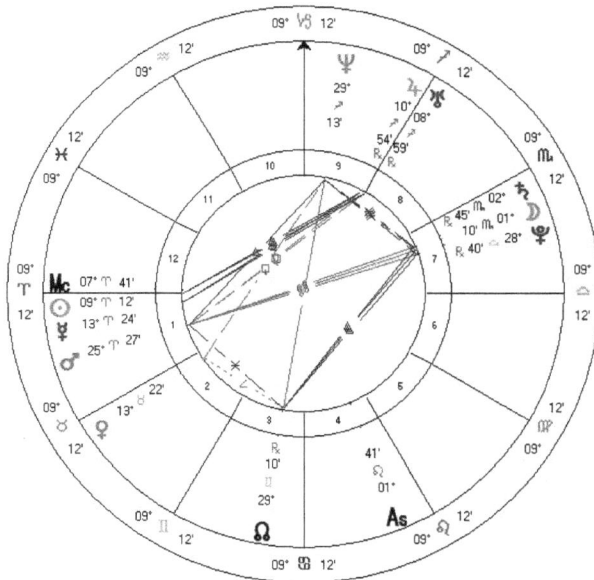

Figure 81 Crude Oil First Trade horoscope

My experience has shown that Crude Oil is a complex instrument to analyze using Astrology. Given the peculiar rectangular shape that appears in the horoscope, my strategy for analyzing Crude Oil has been to use basic McWhirter astrology with a focus on transiting Sun and transiting Mars making 0 degree aspects to the four corner points of the rectangle.

The chart in Figure 82 illustrates Oil price action with events of Sun transiting the four corners of the rectangle overlaid. In my opinion, the event of Sun making a 0 degree aspect to the natal Node position is the most potent of the four corner events. In fact, such an aspect marked the

129

June 2014 price peak and subsequent trend change on Crude Oil. At this time of writing, I note that Crude Oil tried very recently to surpass $62 per barrel. Price failed and the trend turned down right at a Sun/natal Node 0 degree aspect. As further evidence of this aspect's potency, I note to that in 2008, price recorded a double top at or near the $147 per barrel level. The first of these tops came right at a Sun/natal Node 0 degree aspect.

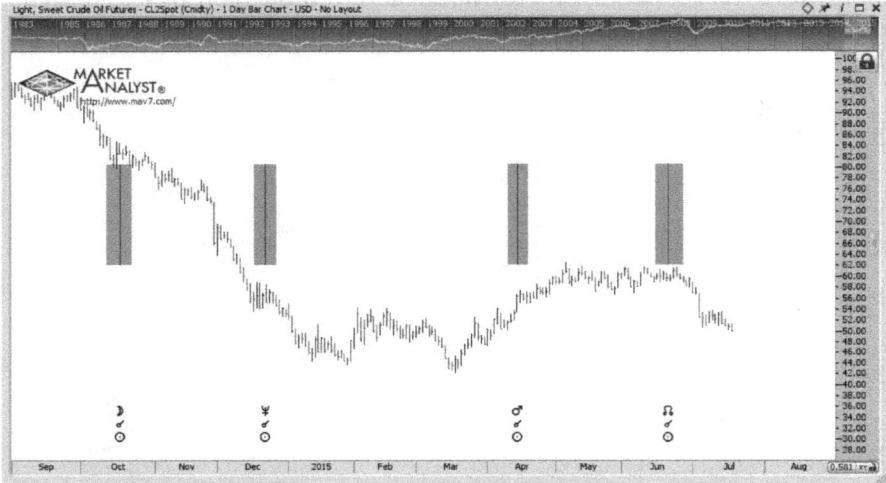

Figure 82 Crude Oil and Sun transits

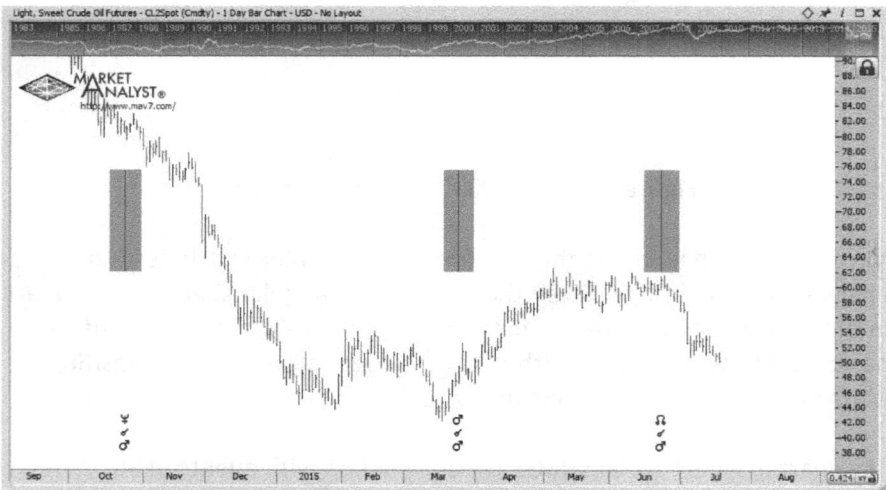

Figure 83 Crude Oil and Mars transits

The chart in Figure 83 illustrates Oil price action with events of Mars transiting the four corners of the rectangle overlaid. In my opinion, the events of Mars making a 0 degree aspect to the natal Node position and Mars making a 0 degree aspect to the natal Mars position are very potent indeed.

For 2016, the four corners of the peculiar rectangle will be aspected as follows:

Sun will transit 0 degrees to the natal Mars location from April 7 through April 22.

Sun will transit 0 degrees to the natal Node location from June 13 through June 30.

Sun will transit 0 degrees to the natal (Saturn/Pluto/Moon) location from October 17 through November 2.

Sun will transit 0 degrees to the natal Neptune location from December 13 through the end of the year.

Mars will transit past the natal (Saturn/Pluto/Moon) location during the first 22 days of January 2015.

Mars will pass the natal Neptune location from September 12 through October 10.

My studies have shown that Crude Oil is influenced by Mercury Retrograde as well. The Crude Oil price chart in Figure 84 illustrates this effect.

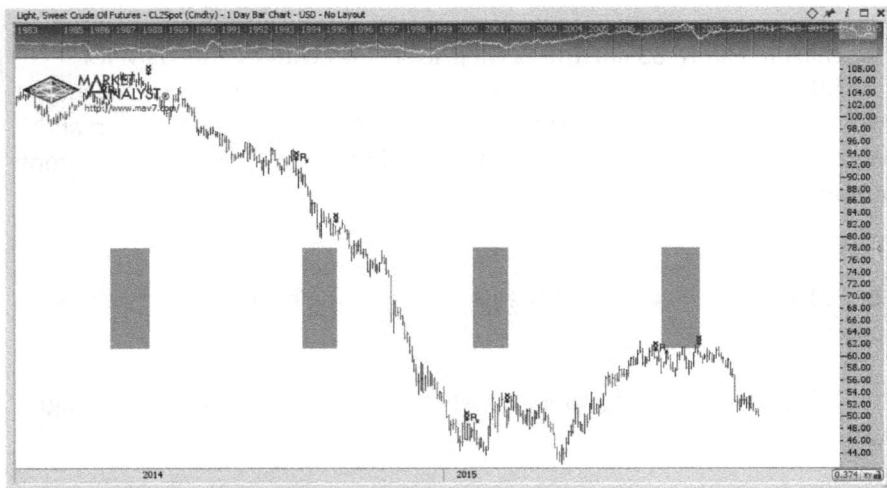

Figure 84 Crude Oil and Mercury Retrograde events

Notice in this chart that he 2014 price peak and subsequent trend change came also at a Retrograde event.

For 2016, Mercury will be Retrograde from:

January 6 through January 25

April 29 through May 22

August 31 through September 22

December 20 through January 9, 2017

Cotton

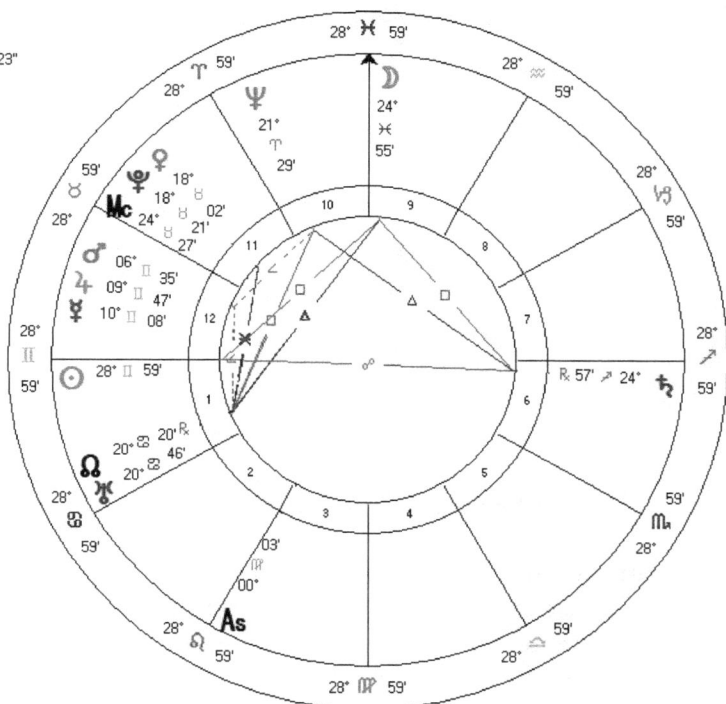

Figure 85 Cotton futures First Trade horoscope

After much painstaking research sifting through back-editions of New York newspapers, I have come to conclude that Cotton futures first started trading on June 20, 1870. The horoscope wheel in Figure 85 illustrates planetary placements at that time. At first glance, I find it peculiar that the Moon is at the same degree and sign location (24 Pisces) as is the Mid-Heaven in the New York Stock Exchange natal horoscope wheel from 1792.

McWhirter astrology events of transiting Sun passing 0, 90 or 180 degrees to the natal Sun position are an effective tool for traders to use when navigating the choppy waters of Cotton prices. A suitable chart technical trend indicator is also a must. The Cotton price chart in Figure 86 illustrates further.

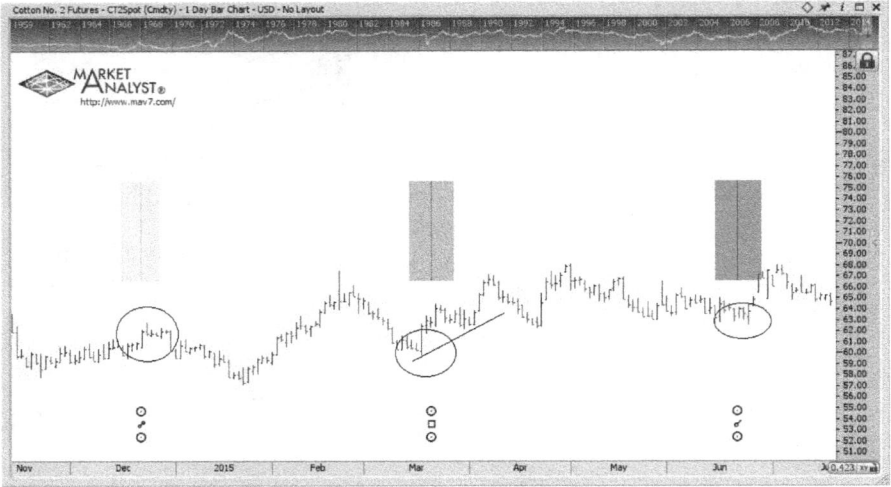

Figure 86 Cotton futures and Sun/natal Sun aspects

One other astro phenomenon traders may wish to consider as a tool to use is the occurrence of Venus passing by the natal Moon position at 24 Pisces. Not a frequent event, it is nonetheless one to pay attention to. The price chart in Figure 87 illustrates.

In 2016, transiting Sun will aspect natal Sun as follows:

Transiting Sun will pass 90 degrees to natal Sun from March 7 through March 23.

Transiting Sun will pass 0 degrees conjunct to natal Sun from June 10 through June 30.

Transiting Sun will pass 90 degrees to natal Sun from September 13 through September 30.

Transiting Sun will pass 180 degrees to natal Sun from December 12 through December 28.

Figure 87 Cotton futures and Venus/natal Moon aspects

During 2016, Venus will transit past the natal Moon position from March 28 through April 5.

Coffee

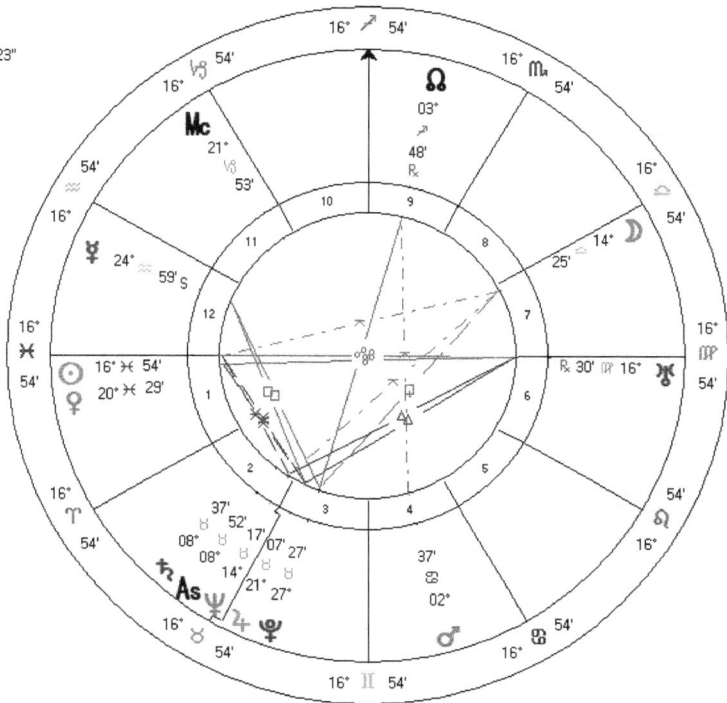

Figure 88 Coffee futures First Trade horoscope

Coffee futures started trading in New York in early March of 1882. The horoscope wheel in Figure 88 illustrates planetary placements at that time.

In the Coffee horoscope, note the 180 degree aspect between Sun and Uranus. The McWhirter methodology cautions that it is not wise to invest in situations where this sort of aspect exists because one will experience many wild ups and downs in price over time. A quick look at a 10 year price chart of Coffee reveals a price range of $0.65/pound to $3.06/pound with many wild swings.

Basic McWhirter astrology provides a good tool to help navigate the volatile Coffee market. The Coffee price chart in Figure 89 has been overlaid with events of transiting Sun making 0, 90 and 180 degree aspects to the natal Sun position at 17 Pisces.

Not each and every aspect event tranlates into a trend change, hence it is necessary to also employ a suitable chart technical indicator as well.

Figure 89 Coffee prices and McWhirter astrology

In 2016, transiting Sun will aspect natal Sun as follows:

Transiting Sun will pass 0 degrees conjunct to natal Sun from February 29 through March 16.

Transiting Sun will pass 90 degrees conjunct to natal Sun from May 31 through June 17.

Transiting Sun will pass 180 degrees to natal Sun from August 31 through September 19.

Transiting Sun will pass 90 degrees to natal Sun from December 10 through December 16.

The positioning of Sun opposite Uranus in the 1882 natal horoscope is intrigiung. It turns out that Sun/Uranus aspects can be used to further assist the trader with decision making. Figure 90 illustrates further.

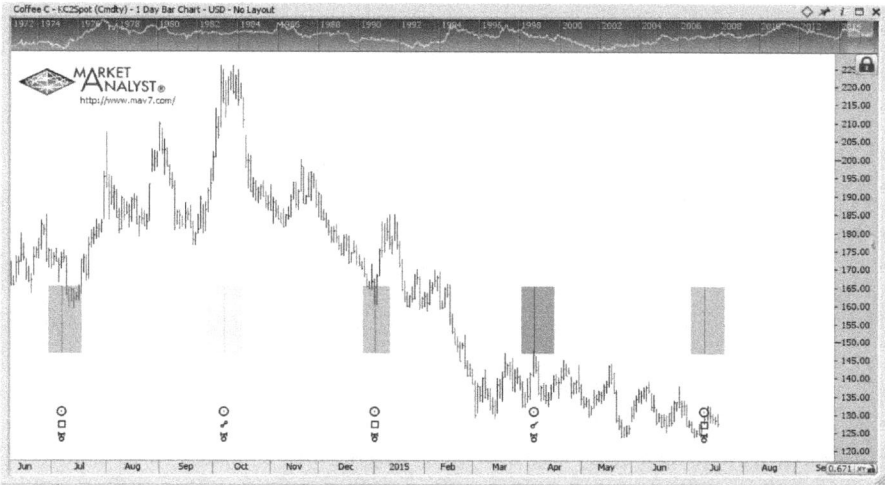

Figure 90 Coffee prices and Sun/Uranus aspects

For 2016, Sun will make hard aspects with Uranus from January 1 through the 13th, from July 10 through July 22nd, and from October 9 through the 21st .

Venus astro events have an effect on price action of Coffee futures. This is likely the case due to the conjunction of Venus and Sun in the First Trade chart horoscope. The Coffee price chart in Figure 91 has been overlaid with Venus-Sun hard aspects as well as two Venus Retrograde events. Note how Coffee prices began to surge immediately as soon as the Venus Retrograde event of early 2014 concluded.

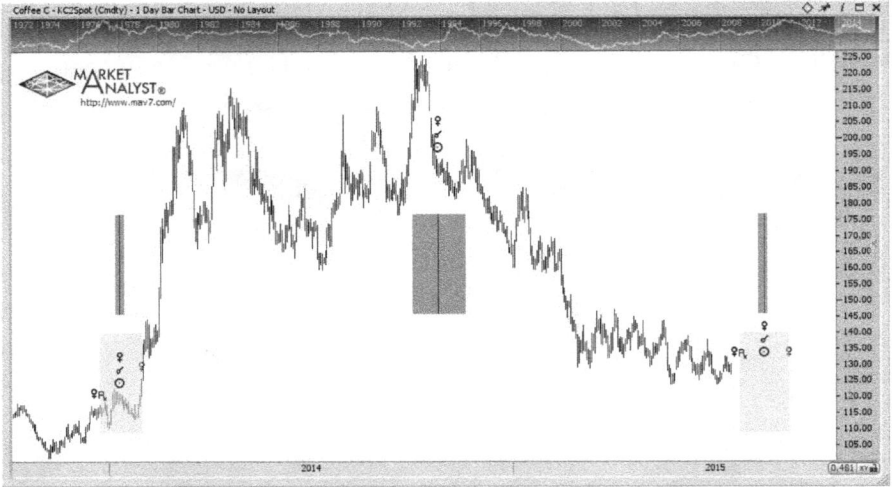

Figure 91 Coffee prices and Venus

For 2016, transiting Venus will make a 0 degree hard aspect to transiting Sun from May 15 through July 9.

Venus will not be Retrograde in 2016.

Lean Hogs

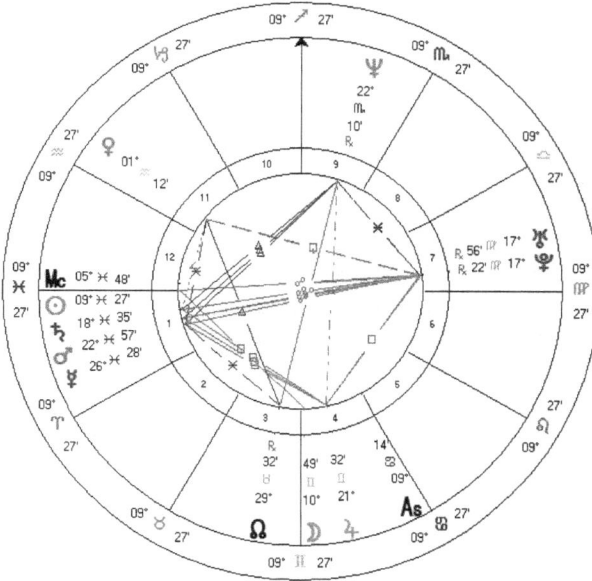

Figure 92 Lean Hogs First Trade horoscope

Lean Hogs futures started trading in Chicago in late February of 1966. The horoscope wheel in Figure 92 illustrates planetary placements at that time.

I have studied Lean Hogs in detail and the most repetitive astro event that I can find that aligns to trend changes is that of Mercury Retrograde. The price chart in Figure 93 illustrates the alignment between Mercury Retrograde and Lean Hogs prices. Traders of Lean Hogs should use a suitable chart technical trend change indicator as these Retrograde events are unfolding.

Figure 93 Lean Hogs prices and Mercury Retrograde events

For 2016, Mercury will be Retrograde from:

January 6 through January 25

April 29 through May 22

August 31 through September 22

December 20 through January 9, 2017

Sugar

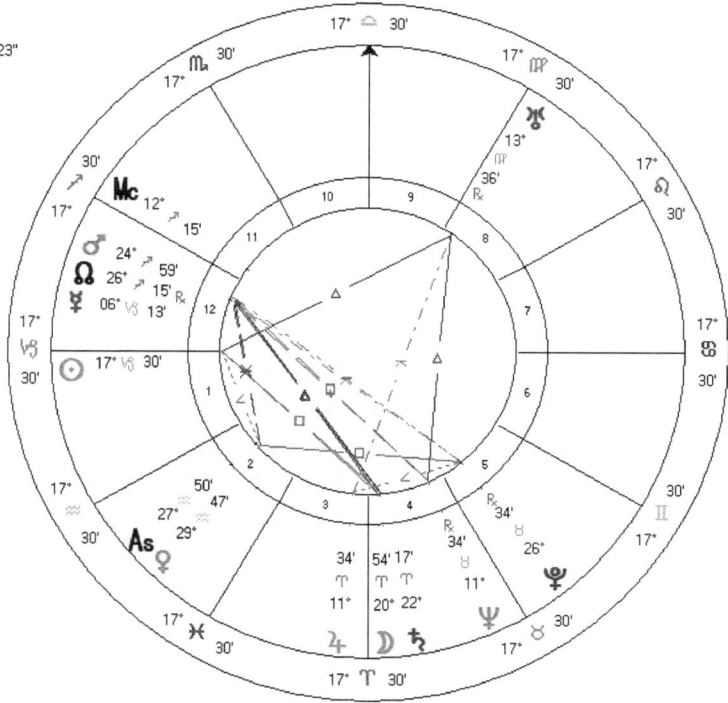

Sugar Futures Natal Chart
7 Jan 1881 NS, Fri
9:30 am EST +5:00
New York, NY
40°N42'51" 074°W00'23"
Geocentric
Tropical
Sun on 1st
Mean Node
Parallax Moon

Figure 94 Sugar Futures First Trade horoscope

Sugar futures started trading in New York in early January of 1881. The horoscope wheel in Figure 94 illustrates planetary placements at that time.

My studies of Sugar futures have shown that McWhirter astrology is very much applicable. In particular, events of transiting Sun making 0,90,120 and 180 degree aspects to the natal Sun location at 17 Capricorn have a high propensity to align to pivot swing points. The price chart in Figure 95 illustrates further.

Figure 95 Sugar prices and McWhirter astrology

For 2016, transiting Sun will make a 0 degree aspect to natal Sun from January 4 through January 14. Transiting Sun will make a 90 degree aspect to natal Sun from April 1 through April 12. A 120 degree aspect will be seen from May 2 through May 13. A 180 degree aspect will occur from July 4 through July 15. A 90 degree aspect will occur from October 5 through October 21.

Mercury Retrograde events also align to short term trend changes on Sugar price as the chart in Figure 96 illustrates.

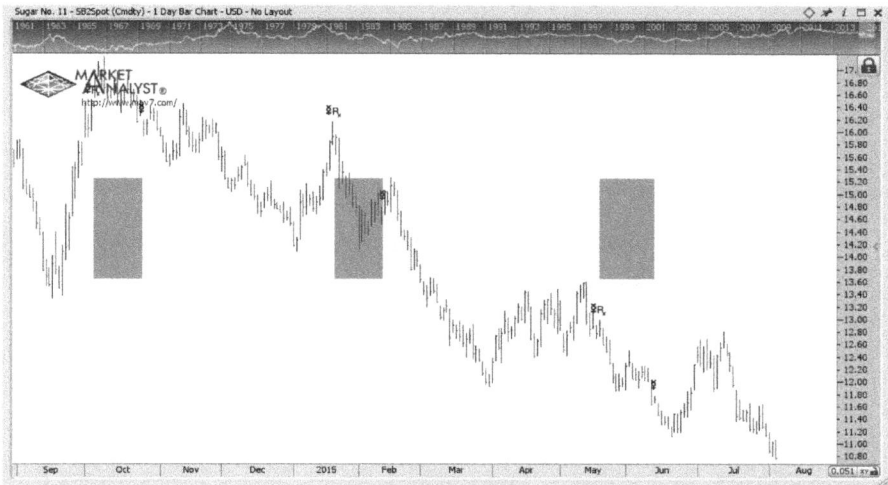

Figure 96 Mercury Retrograde and Sugar price

For 2016, Mercury will be Retrograde from:

January 6 through January 25

April 29 through May 22

August 31 through September 22

December 20 through January 9, 2017

Cocoa

Cocoa futures started trading in New York in early October 1925. The horoscope wheel in Figure 97 illustrates planetary placements at that time.

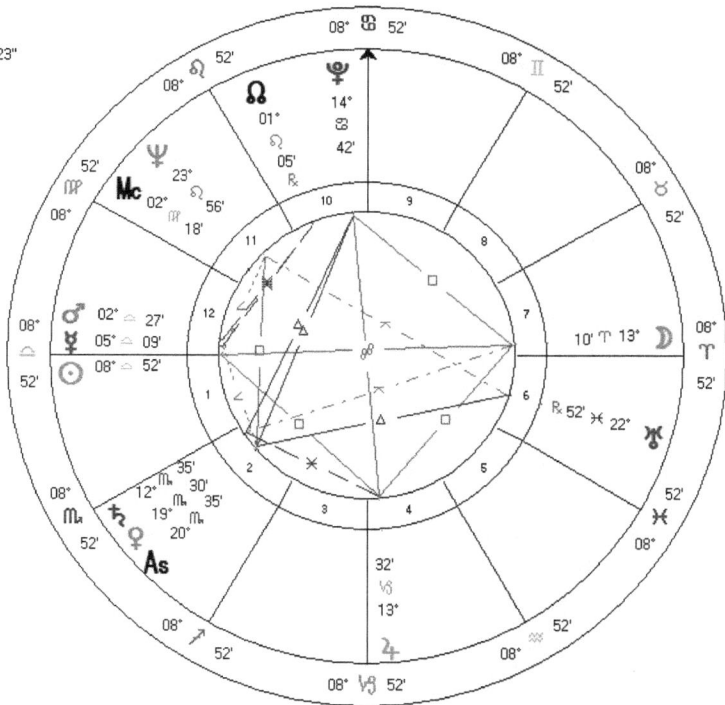

Figure 97 Cocoa futures First Trade horoscope

Mercury Retrograde events have a high propensity to align to pivot swing points on Cocoa price. The price chart in Figure 98 illustrates further.

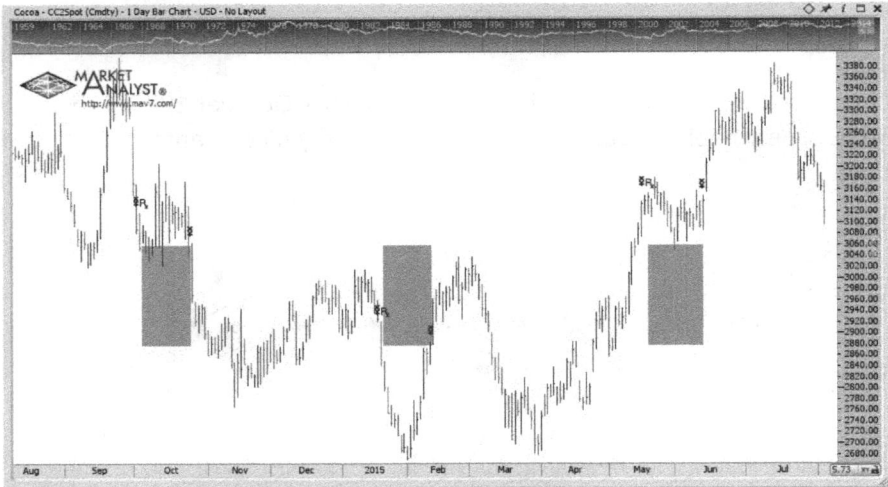

Figure 98 Mercury Retrograde and Cocoa price

For 2016, Mercury will be Retrograde from:

January 6 through January 25

April 29 through May 22

August 31 through September 22

December 20 through January 9, 2017

The 1925 natal horoscope shows Sun and Mercury conjunct (0 degrees apart). My research has shown that events of Mercury being at its maximum easterly and westerly elongations and events of Mercury being at its Inferior and Superior conjunctions align quite well to pivot swing points. The price chart in Figure 99 illustrates further.

Figure 99 Cocoa price and Mercury cycles

For 2016, Mercury will be at its maximum easterly elongation on April 18, August 16 and again on December 11. Mercury will be at its maximum westerly elongations on February 7, June 5 and September 28.

During 2016, Mercury will be at Inferior Conjunction on January 14, May 9, September 13 and December 28. Mercury will be at Superior Conjunction on March 23, July 7 and October 27.

7. ESOTERIC MATH TECHNIQUES

Gann Fan Lines

Gann lines are a technique in which a starting point of a significant high or low is selected. From this point, angles (vectors) are projected outwards. These vectors are the 1x1, 1x2, 1x4, 1x8 and the 2x1, 4x1 and 8x1.

Many market data software platforms will come with a Gann Fan function already built in. The confusion with Gann lines comes from the mathematical method of constructing the lines. My preference is the methodology used by Daniel Ferrera in his book *Gann for the Active Trader*. Ferrera's method is based on the Gann Square of Nine mathematics.

To illustrate the creation of Gann lines, I am going to use Gold as an example. On March 17, 2014, Gold made a price high at $1392. This is the point from which I wish to extend Gann lines.

Step 1: Take the $1392 and express it simply as the number 1392. Take the square root of the number 1392 and you get 37.3. This will be your time factor.

Step 2: Subtract 1 from 37.3 and re-square this figure to get 1318.

Step 3: We can now state that our time factor is 37.3 calendar days. We can further state that our price factor is 1392 minus 1318 = $74.

Step 4: From the March 17 date, you will extend a line so that it passes through the time co-ordinate (March 17+37.3 days = April 23) and the price co-ordinate $1318. This line is the Gann 1x1 line.

Step 5: From the March 17 date, you will extend a line so that it passes through the time co-ordinate (March 17+(37.3 x 2) days = May 30) and the price co-ordinate $1318. This line is the Gann 1x2 line.

Step 6: From the March 17 date, you will extend a line so that it passes through the time co-ordinate ((March 17+(0.5)*37.32)days = April 4) and the price co-ordinate $1318. This line is the Gann 2x1 line.

Step 7: From the March 17 date, you will extend a line so that it passes through the time co-ordinate ((March 17+(0.25)*37.32)days = March 26) and the price co-ordinate $1318. This line is the Gann 4x1 line.

The Gold price chart in Figure 100 has these Gann lines overlaid starting from the March $1392 high. This chart has been prepared in the Market Analyst software platform.

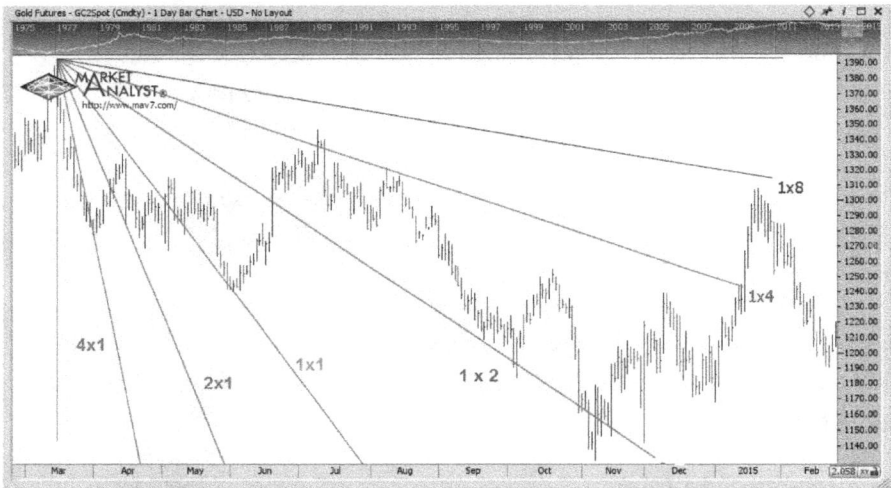

Figure 100 Gann Lines applied to a Gold Chart

Notice from the $1392 high, price action dropped, following the 4x1 line. A rally then pushed price up to the 1x1 line. The rally failed and price fell back to the 2x1 line. A sideways consolidation then ensued for several weeks. A price low was registered right at the 1x1 line. Price then rallied up through the 1x2 line and hit resistance at the 1x4 line. Price then drifted lower and eventually recorded a significant low in the November 2014 timeframe just a bit underneath the 1x2 line. In early 2015, a rally failed just shy of the 1x8 line. At this time of this chart was created in early August 2015, Gold price was in a downtrend, with overhead resistance at the 1x4 line at the $1100 level.

To further illustrate Gann Fan lines, consider the price action of Crude Oil which registered a significant high on June 20, 2014 ay $107.73.

Step 1: Take the $107.73 and express it simply as the number 1077.3. Take the square root of the number 1077.3 and you get 32.8. This will be your time factor.

Step 2: Subtract 1 from 32.8 and re-square this figure to get 1011.24.

Step 3: We can now state that our time factor is 32.8 calendar days. We can further state that our price factor is 1077 minus 1011 = $66.

Step 4: From the June 20 date, you will extend a line so that it passes through the time co-ordinate (June 20 +32.8 days = July 23) and the price co-ordinate $1011. This line is the Gann 1x1 line.

Step 5: From the June 20 date, you will extend a line so that it passes through the time co-ordinate (June 20+(32.8 x 2) days = August 25) and the price co-ordinate $1011. This line is the Gann 1x2 line.

Next, consider that Crude Oil made a significant low on March 18, 2015 at the $42.30 level.

Step 1: Take the $42.30 level and express it simply as the number 423.0. Take the square root of the number 423.0 and you get 20.56. This will be your time factor.

Step 2: Add 1 to 20.56 and re-square this figure to get 464.83.

Step 3: We can now state that our time factor is 20.56 calendar days. We can further state that our price factor is 464 minus 423 = $41.

Step 4: From the March 18 date, you will extend a line so that it passes through the time co-ordinate (March 18 +20.5 days = April 8) and the price co-ordinate $46.48. This line is the Gann 1x1 line.

Step 5: From the March 18 date, you will extend a line so that it passes through the time co-ordinate (March 18 + (20.56 x 2) days = April 29) and the price co-ordinate $46.48. This line is the Gann 1x2 line.

Step 6: From the March 18 date, you will extend a line so that it passes through the time co-ordinate (March 18 + (20.56 x 8) days = August 31) and the price co-ordinate $46.48. This line is the Gann 1x8 line.

And there you go. The math is really quite straightforward for all of the Gann Fan lines once you identify the starting point and use Ferrera's method involving squares and square roots.

The Crude Oil price chart in Figure 101 has these Gann lines overlaid starting from the June $107.73 high. This chart too has been prepared in Market Analyst using the built-in Gann Fan function based on Ferrera's approach. As I craft this part of the manuscript in August 2015, I note that Oil price is hovering just above the 1x8 line and the prevailing trend is to the downside.

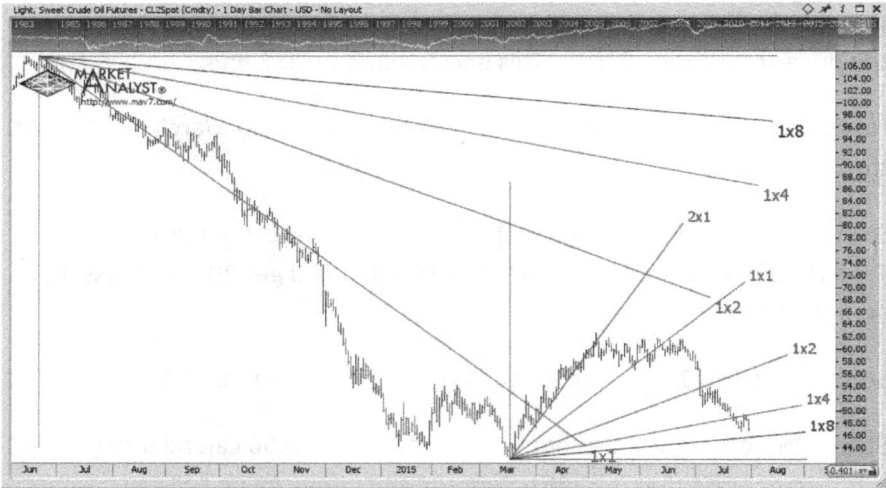

Figure 101 Crude Oil with Gann Fans

Gann Planetary Transit Lines

There is one astrological technique whose power continues to amaze me. The technique I refer to is Gann Planetary Transit Lines. (For a detailed description of how to construct Transit Lines, see my second book, *The Lost Science* or see Jeanne Long's book, *The Universal Clock*. The construction methodology is quite simple and either of these publications will step you through it).

Transit lines involve taking the longitudinal position of a given planet and converting that longitude to price by means of the Wheel of 24 (also known as the Universal Clock). Typically, transit lines are plotted for Mars, Jupiter, Saturn, Uranus and Neptune. Once the transit lines have been calculated and plotted, one can then overlay price data on the chart.

Figure 102 illustrates a chart of Crude Oil prices I have added the Uranus transit lines. This chart has been prepared in the Market Analyst software platform using the built-in Gann Planetary Transit function.

Notice how price highs in each of 2011, 2012, 2013 and 2014 came in very close conjunction to one of the Uranus transit lines. As I craft this part of the manuscript in August 2015, the trend on Crude Oil is to the downside and a Uranus transit line at the $38 level is offering support.

The Market Analyst platform has a built-in planetary transit line function that is as simple as the click of a mouse.

Figure 102 Crude Oil and Uranus Transit Lines

To further illustrate the power of transit lines, consider the chart in Figure 103 of the Dow Jones Industrial Average. Note how the general slope of the Dow Jones has been following the general slope of the Mars transit lines. Amazing!

Figure 103 Dow Jones Average and Mars Transit Lines

Quantum Price Lines

In the early 1700s and scientist Sir Isaac Newton developed his theory of Universal Gravitation in which he said planets in our solar system are attracted to one another by gravity. Newton also said that space and time were absolute and that the world functioned according to an absolute order. Furthermore, he said that space was a three-dimensional entity and time was a two-dimensional entity.

In the early 1900's, Albert Einstein advanced his theory of Relativity that posited Newton's absolute model was outdated. Einstein said the passage of time of an object was related to its speed with respect to that of another observer. Thus was penned the concept of relative space- time in which space was not uniform.

Einstein further stated that relative space-time could be distorted depending on the density of matter. That is, space-time in the area of the Sun is more distorted because the Sun has a great, huge mass. Light particles travelling near the Sun are then distorted from their linear path due to the mass of the Sun.

Quantum Price Lines are based on this quantum theory. The whole notion of quantum lines posits that the price of a stock, index or commodity can be thought of as a light particle or electron that can occupy different energy levels or orbital shells.

Author Fabio Oreste has done a masterful job of taking quantum physics, blending it with the curvature mathematics of Riemann and applying the whole thing to price charting. Price is considered to be akin to light particles. These light particles are then deflected by actions of planets. This deflection is what gives us price highs and lows on a chart.

Essentially, what Oreste has done is take the Gann Transit Line notion and marry it to modern physics and bring it into the 21st century. Oreste's book is entitled *Quantum Trading* and is available through most on-line book-sellers. No trader's bookshelf should be without it.

The Oreste formula for quantum price line calculation is :

Quantum Line = (N x 360) + PSO ;

Where PSO = heliocentric planetary longitude x Conversion Scale
Where N= the harmonic level
Where Conversion Scale = 2^n ; 1,2,4,8,16 ….

When dealing with prices less than 360, the inverse variation of the formula is used.

Quantum LIne = (1/N x 360) + PSO

To go into a lengthy description of quantum lines would quickly double the size of this manuscript. In the interest of brevity, what follows is a listing of the harmonic lines you may wish to overlay onto your various charts for 2016. You may be shocked to find how price action tends to closely respect these harmonics and sub-harmonics. Give some thought to obtaining Oreste's book if you wish to delve deeper.

S&P500 Index

I have found that the **Pluto** quantum lines (Conversion Scale =2, N=2) work quite well for the S&P 500 Index. During 2016, consider drawing the following suite of quantum lines onto your daily chart of the S&P500 Index. Each line should start at January 1, 2016 and terminate at December 31, 2016.

January 2016	December 2016
1451	1456
1532	1537
1613	1618
1693	1698
1774	1779
1854	1860
1935	1941
2016	2022
2096	2103
2177	2184
2258	2265
2338	2345
2419	2426

Nasdaq Composite Index

I have found that the **Pluto** quantum lines (Conversion Scale =8, N=2) work quite well for the Nasdaq Composite. During 2016, consider drawing the following suite of quantum lines onto your daily chart of the Nasdaq Composite. Each line should start at January 1, 2016 and terminate at December 31, 2016.

January 2016	December 2016
3928	3959
4125	4147
4313	4336
4500	4524
4688	4713
4875	4901
5063	5090
5250	5278
5438	5467
5625	5655
5813	5844

Dow Jones Industrial Average

I have found that the **Pluto** quantum lines (Conversion Scale =32, N=2) work quite well for the Dow Jones Average. During 2016, consider drawing the following suite of quantum lines onto your daily chart of the Dow. Each line should start at January 1, 2016 and terminate at December 31, 2016.

January 2016	December 2016
14760	14856
15375	15475
15990	16094
16605	16713
17720	17332
17835	17951
18450	18750
19065	19189

FTSE 100 Index

I have found that the **Pluto** quantum lines (Conversion Scale =16, N=2) work quite well for the FTSE 100. During 2016, consider drawing the following suite of quantum lines onto your daily chart of the FTSE. Each line should start at January 1, 2016 and terminate at December 31, 2016.

January 2016	December 2016
5940	5976
6270	6308
6600	6640
6930	6972
7260	7304
7590	7636
7920	7968

German DAX Index

I have found that the **Pluto** quantum lines (Conversion Scale=16 & 32, N=2) work quite well for the DAX. During 2016, consider drawing the following suite of quantum lines onto your daily chart of the DAX. Each line should start at January 1, 2016 and terminate at December 31, 2016.

January 2016	December 2016
7920	7968
8250	8300
8580	8632
8910	8964
9240	9296
9570	9628
9900	9960
10230	10292
10455	10523
11070	11142
11685	11761
12300	12380

January 2016	December 2016
12915	12999
13530	13618
14145	14237
14760	14856

Gold Futures

I have found that the **Pluto** quantum lines (Conversion Scale=1, N=2) work quite well for Gold. During 2016, consider drawing the following suite of quantum lines onto your daily chart of Gold. Each line should start at January 1, 2016 and terminate at December 31, 2016.
.

January 2016	December 2016
1005	1007
1131	1133
1193	1196
1256	1259
1319	1322
1382	1385
1445	1448
1508	1511
1570	1573
1633	1636
1696	1699
1759	1762

Silver Futures

I have found that the **Pluto** quantum lines (Conversion Scale=1/64, N=1/64) work quite well for Silver. During 2016, consider drawing the following suite of quantum lines onto your daily chart of Silver. Each line should start at January 1, 2016 and terminate at December 31, 2016.

January 2016	December 2016
10.06	10.09
10.68	10.72
11.32	11.35
11.95	11.99
12.58	12.62
13.21	13.25
13.84	13.88
14.46	14.51
15.09	15.14
15.72	15.77
16.35	16.40
16.98	17.03
17.61	17.66
18.24	18.29
18.87	18.92
19.50	19.56

Currency Futures (Canadian Dollar, Australian Dollar, Japanese Yen)

I have found that the **Pluto** quantum lines (Conversion Scale=1/1024, N=1/1024) work quite well for these currencies. During 2016, consider drawing the following suite of quantum lines onto your daily chart of each of these currencies. Each line should start at January 1, 2016 and terminate at December 31, 2016

January 2016	December 2016
0.6321	0.6340
0.6716	0.6737
0.7111	0.7133
0.7506	0.7529
0.7901	0.7926
0.8296	0.8322
0.8691	0.8718
0.9086	0.9115
0.9482	0.9511
0.9877	0.9907
1.0272	1.0303

Currency Futures (Euro and British Pound)

I have found that the **Pluto** quantum lines (Conversion Scale=1/1024 & 1/512, N=1/1024 & 1/512) work quite well for these currencies. During 2016, consider drawing the following suite of quantum lines onto your daily chart of each of these currencies. Each line should start at January 1, 2016 and terminate at December 31, 2016

January 2016	December 2016
0.9482	0.9511
0.9877	0.9907
1.0272	1.0303
1.0667	1.0700
1.1062	1.1096
1.1457	1.1492
1.1852	1.1889
1.2247	1.2285
1.2577	1.2616
1.3363	1.3405
1.4150	1.4194
1.4936	1.4982
1.5722	1.5771
1.6508	1.6559
1.7294	1.7348
1.8080	1.8136
1.8866	1.8925
1.9652	1.9713

Wheat and Corn Futures

I have found that the **Pluto** quantum lines (Conversion Scale=1/256 & 1/128, N=1/256 & 1/128) work quite well for these currencies. During 2016, consider drawing the following suite of quantum lines onto your daily chart of each of these grains. Each line should start at January 1, 2016 and terminate at December 31, 2016.

January 2016	December 2016
2.82	2,83
2.98	2.99
3.14	3.15
3.30	3.31
3.45	3.46
3.61	3.62
3.77	3.78
3.93	3.94
4.08	4.10
4.24	4.25
4.40	4.41
4.55	4.57
4.71	4.73
4.87	4.88
5.03	5.04
5.34	5.35
5.65	5.67
5.97	5.99
6.28	6.30
6.60	6.62
6.91	6.93
7.23	7.25
7.54	7.57
7.86	7.88

Soybean Futures

I have found that the **Pluto** quantum lines (Conversion Scale=1/64 & 1/128, N=1/64 & 1/128) work quite well for Beans. During 2016, consider drawing the following suite of quantum lines onto your daily chart of Beans. Each line should start at January 1, 2016 and terminate at December 31, 2016.

January 2016	December 2016
8.80	8.83
9.11	9.14
9.43	9.46
9.74	9.77
10.06	10.09
10.68	10.72
11.32	11.35
11.94	11.98
12.57	12.61
13.20	13.24
13.83	13.87
14.46	14.50
15.09	15.13
15.72	15.77
16.35	16.40
16.97	17.03

Crude Oil Futures

I have found that the **Pluto** quantum lines (Conversion Scale=1/16, N=1/16) work quite well for Oil. During 2016, consider drawing the following suite of quantum lines onto your daily chart of Oil. Each line should start at January 1, 2016 and terminate at December 31, 2016.

January 2016	December 2016
40.31	42.43
42.82	42.95
45.35	45.49
47.87	48.01
50.39	50.54
52.91	53.07
55.42	55.60
57.94	58.12
60.46	60.65
62.98	63.18
65.50	67.71
68.02	68.23
70.54	70.76
73.06	73.29
75.58	75.82
78.10	78.34

The Script Tool function in Market Analyst works exceptionally well for creating Quantum Price lines to overlay onto price charts.

30 Year Bond Futures

I have found that the **Saturn** quantum lines (Conversion Scale=1/4 & 1/8, N=1/4 & 1/8) work quite well for Bonds. During 2016, consider drawing the following suite of quantum lines onto your daily chart of Bonds. Each line should start at January 1, 2016 and terminate at December 31, 2016.

January 2016	December 2016
133.00	135.18
137.75	140.01
142.5	144.84
147.25	149.67
152	154.5
161.50	164.15
171	173.81
180.5	183.46

10 Year Treasury Note Futures

I have found that the **Pluto** quantum lines (Conversion Scale=1/8, N=1/8) work quite well for Treasuries. During 2016, consider drawing the following suite of quantum lines onto your daily chart of Treasuries. Each line should start at January 1, 2016 and terminate at December 31, 2016.

January 2016	December 2016
118.75	120.70
123.5	125.53
128.25	130.35
133.00	135.18
137.75	140.01

Sugar Futures

I have found that the **Pluto** quantum lines (Conversion Scale = 1/64 and 1/32). During 2016, consider drawing the following suite of quantum lines onto your daily chart of Sugar prices. Each line should start at January 1, 2016 and terminate at December 31, 2016.

January 2016	December 2016
26.166	26.597
23.788	24.179
21.409	21.761
19.030	19.343
17.784	18.076
16.598	16.871
15.412	15.666
14.227	14.461
13.041	13.256
11.856	12.051
10.670	10.845

Cocoa Futures

I have found that the **Pluto** quantum lines (Conversion Scale=4 & 8, N=2) work quite well for Cocoa. During 2016, consider drawing the following suite of quantum lines onto your daily chart of Cocoa. Each line should start at January 1, 2016 and terminate at December 31, 2016.

January 2016	December 2016
3549	3654
3380	3480
3211	3306
3042	3132
2704	2784
2568	2628
2461	2518
2354	2409
2247	2299
2140	2190
2033	2080

8. EPILOGUE

I have taken you on a wide ranging journey in this Almanac to acquaint you with the mathematical and astrological links between investor emotion and market behavior. I sincerely hope you will embrace Financial Astrology as a valuable tool to assist you in your trading and investing activity. I further hope you will pause often to reflect on the deeper connection between the financial markets, Astrology and the emotions of mankind.

On that note, I will leave you with the words of Neil Turok from his 2012 book, *The Universe Within*.

"Perseverance leads to enlightenment. And the truth is more beautiful than your wildest dreams".

9. GLOSSARY OF TERMS

Ascendant: One of four cardinal points on a horoscope, the Ascendant is situated in the East

Aspect: The angular relationship between two planets measured in degrees

Autumnal Equinox: (see Equinox) – That time of year when Sun is at 0 degrees Libra

Conjunct: An angular relationship of 0 degrees between two planets

Cosmo-biology: Changes in human emotion caused by changes in cosmic energy

Descendant: One of four cardinal points on a horoscope, the Descendant is situated in the West

Ephemeris: A daily tabular compilation of planetary and lunar positions

Equinox: An event occurring twice annually, an equinox event marks the time when the tilt of the Earth's axis is neither toward or away from the Sun

First Trade chart: A zodiac chart depicting the positions of the planets at the time a company's stock or a commodity future commenced trading on a recognized financial exchange

First Trade date: The date a stock or commodity futures contract first began trading on a recognized exchange

Full Moon: From a vantage point situated on Earth, when the Moon is seen to be 180 degrees to the Sun

Geocentric Astrology: That version of Astrology in which the vantage point for determining planetary aspects is the Earth

Heliocentric Astrology: That version of Astrology in which the vantage point for determining planetary aspects is the Sun

House: A 1/12th portion of the zodiac. Portions are not necessarily equal depending on the mathematical formula used to calculate the divisions

Lunar Eclipse: A lunar eclipse occurs when the Sun, Earth, and Moon are aligned exactly, or very closely so, with the Earth in the middle. The Earth blocks the Sun's rays from striking the Moon.

Lunar Month: (see Synodic Month)

Lunation: (see New Moon)

Mid-Heaven: One of four cardinal points on a horoscope, the Mid-Heaven is situated in the South

New Moon: From a vantage point situated on Earth, when the Moon is seen to be 0 degrees to the Sun

North Node of Moon: The intersection points between the Moon's plane and Earth's ecliptic are termed the North and South nodes. Astrologers tend to focus on the North node and Ephemeris tables clearly list the zodiacal position of the North Node for each calendar day

Orb: The amount of flexibility or tolerance given to an aspect

Retrograde motion: The apparent backwards motion of a planet through the zodiac signs when viewed from a vantage point on Earth

Sidereal Month: The Moon orbits Earth with a slightly elliptical pattern in approximately 27.3 days, relative to a fixed frame of reference.

Sidereal Orbital Period: The time required for a planet to make one full orbit of the Sun as viewed from a fixed vantage point on the Sun

Siderograph: A mathematical equation developed by astrologer Donald Bradley in 1946 (By plotting the output of the equation against date, inflection points can be seen on the plotted curve. It is at these inflection points that human emotion is most apt to change resulting in a trend change on the Dow Jones or S&P 500 Index)

Solar Eclipse: A solar eclipse occurs when the Moon passes between the Sun and Earth and fully or partially blocks the Sun.

Solstice: Occurring twice annually, a solstice event marks the time when the Sun reaches its highest or lowest altitude above the horizon at noon.

Stationary: A planet is said to be stationary the day before it turns Retrograde and also the day before it goes from being Retrograde to being Direct.

Synodic Month: During a sidereal month (see Sidereal Month), Earth will revolve part way around the Sun thus making the average apparent time between one New Moon and the next New Moon longer than the sidereal month at approximately 29.5 days. This 29.5 day time span is called a Synodic Month or sometimes a Lunar Month.

Synodic Orbital Period: The time required for a planet to make one full orbit of the Sun as viewed from a fixed vantage point on Earth

Vernal Equinox: That time of the year when Sun is at 0 degrees Aries.

Zodiac: An imaginary band encircling the 360 degrees of the planetary system divided into twelve equal portions of 30 degrees each

Zodiac Wheel: A circular image broken into 12 portions of 30 degrees each. Each portion represents a different astrological sign

10. OTHER BOOKS BY THE AUTHOR

Once maligned by many, the subject of financial Astrology is now experiencing a revival as traders and investors seek deeper insight into the forces that move the financial markets.

The markets are a dynamic entity fueled by many factors, some of which we can easily comprehend, some of which are esoteric. This book introduces the reader to the notion that astrological phenomena can influence price action on financial markets and create trend changes across both short and longer term time horizons. From an introduction to the historical basics behind Astrology through to an examination of lunar Astrology and planetary aspects, the numerous illustrated examples in this book will introduce the reader the power of Astrology and its impact on both equity markets and commodity futures markets.

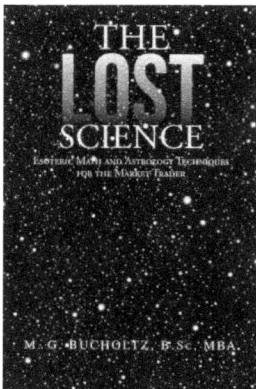

The financial markets are a reflection of the psychological emotions of traders and investors. These emotions ebb and flow in harmony with the forces of nature.

Scientific techniques and phenomena such as square root mathematics, the Golden Mean, the Golden Sequence, lunar events, planetary transits and planetary aspects have been used by civilizations dating as far back as the ancient Egyptians in order to comprehend the forces of nature.

The emotions of traders and investors can be seen to fluctuate in accordance with these forces of nature. Lunar events can be seen to align with trend changes on financial markets. Significant market cycles can be seen to align with planetary transits and aspects. Price patterns on stocks, commodity futures and market indices can be seen to conform to square root and Golden Mean mathematics.

In the early years of the 20th century the most successful traders on Wall Street, including the venerable W.D. Gann, used these scientific techniques and phenomena to profit from the markets. However, over the ensuing decades as technology has advanced, the science has been lost.

The Lost Science acquaints the reader with an extensive range of astrological and mathematical phenomena. From the Golden Mean and Fibonacci Sequence, to planetary transit lines and square roots through to an examination of lunar Astrology and planetary aspects, the numerous illustrated examples in this book will show the reader how these unique scientific phenomena impact the financial markets.

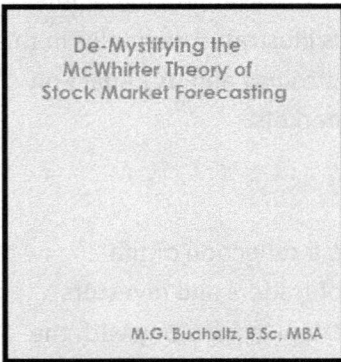

De-Mystifying the
McWhirter Theory of
Stock Market Forecasting

M.G. Bucholtz, B.Sc, MBA

Very little is known about Louise McWhirter, except that in 1937 she wrote the book *McWhirter Theory of Stock Market Forecasting.*

In my travels to places as far away as the British Library in London, England to research financial Astrology, not once did I come across any other books by her. Not once did I find any other book from her era that even mentioned her name. All of this I find to be deeply mysterious. Whoever she was – she wrote only one book, and it was a powerful one that is as accurate today as it was back in 1937. The purpose of writing this book is suggested by the title itself – to de-mystify McWhirter's methodology - which is not exactly straightforward.

11. ABOUT THE AUTHOR

Malcolm Bucholtz, B.Sc, MBA is a graduate of Queen's University Faculty of Engineering in Canada and Heriot Watt University in Scotland where he received an MBA degree. After working in Canadian industry for far too many years, Malcolm followed his passion for the financial markets by becoming an Investment Advisor/Commodity Trading Advisor with an independent brokerage firm in western Canada. Today, he resides in western Canada where he trades the financial markets using technical chart analysis, esoteric mathematics and the astrological principles outlined in this book.

Malcolm is the author of several books. His first book, *The Bull, the Bear and the Planets*, offers the reader an introduction to Financial Astrology and makes the case that there are esoteric and astrological phenomena that influence the financial markets. His second book, *The Lost Science*, takes the reader on a deeper journey into planetary events and unique mathematical phenomena that influence financial markets. His third book, *De-Mystifying the McWhirter Theory of Stock Market Forecasting* seeks to simplify and illustrate the McWhirter methodology. Malcolm has been writing the Astrology Almanac each year since 2014.

Malcolm maintains both a website (www.investingsuccess.ca) and a blog where he provides traders and investors with astrological insights into the financial markets. He also offers a bi-weekly **Astrology E-Alert** service where subscribers receive previews of pending astrological events that stand to influence markets and cause trend changes.

www.ingramcontent.com/pod-product-compliance
Lightning Source LLC
Chambersburg PA
CBHW050102210326
41519CB00015BA/3796